NOT SO
VIRTUOUS
VICTORIANS

For Mum and Dad

NOT SO VIRTUOUS VICTORIANS

MICHELLE ROSENBERG

PEN & SWORD
HISTORY

AN IMPRINT OF PEN & SWORD BOOKS LTD
YORKSHIRE · PHILADELPHIA

First published in Great Britain in 2021 by
PEN AND SWORD HISTORY
An imprint of
Pen & Sword Books Ltd
Yorkshire – Philadelphia

ISBN 978 1 52670 091 9

Typeset in Times New Roman 12/16 by
SJmagic DESIGN SERVICES, India.
Printed and bound by CPI Group (UK) Ltd, Croydon, CR0 4YY

Pen & Sword Books Limited incorporates the imprints of Atlas, Archaeology,
Aviation, Discovery, Family History, Fiction, History, Maritime, Military,
Military Classics, Politics, Select, Transport, True Crime, Air World,
Frontline Publishing, Leo Cooper, Remember When, Seaforth Publishing,
The Praetorian Press, Wharncliffe Local History, Wharncliffe Transport,
Wharncliffe True Crime and White Owl.

For a complete list of Pen & Sword titles please contact
PEN & SWORD BOOKS LIMITED
47 Church Street, Barnsley, South Yorkshire, S70 2AS, England
E-mail: enquiries@pen-and-sword.co.uk
Website: www.pen-and-sword.co.uk

Or
PEN AND SWORD BOOKS
1950 Lawrence Rd, Havertown, PA 19083, USA
E-mail: Uspen-and-sword@casematepublishers.com
Website: www.penandswordbooks.com

Contents

Introduction

Queen Victoria, who reigned from 1837 to 1901. (*National Portrait Gallery*)

The Victorian era was the period of Queen Victoria's reign, from 20 June 1837 until her death on 22 January 1901.

Ruled over by a 4ft 11ins indomitable queen, the Victorian age was a time of economic growth, progress, rapid industrialisation, technological advancements including the first telephone and telegraph, improved literacy, political reform and social change. It welcomed luminaries including Charles Darwin and Charles Dickens.

History has often lifted the Victorians onto a pedestal of peace, purity and prosperity. *Not So Virtuous Victorians* offers a tantalising look behind that veil: at repressive fashion, prostitution, child labour, sexuality and murder.

Coming to the throne after the death of her uncle William IV, Victoria's reign lasted sixty-four years. Up until recently, when she was surpassed by her great-great granddaughter, Queen Elizabeth II, she was the longest-reigning British monarch.

The Victorian era saw events ranging from the Irish Potato Famine (1845 – 1849), the publication of Karl Marx's *Communist Manifesto* (1848), the Crimean War (1853 – 1856), The Great Exhibition at Crystal Palace in Hyde Park, London (opened 1 May 1851), Big Ben (started 1843 and opened 1859), and the first transatlantic cable (1858). Charles Darwin published *On the Origin of the Species* (1859) and Jack the Ripper terrorised Whitechapel (1888 – 1891).

Women's rights improved under Victoria's reign. They were given limited power to retain their property after marriage – rather than their husband securing all rights automatically. Women were also permitted to keep up to £200 of their own earnings and, on 1 January 1883, married women were allowed to buy their own property.

This book offers a snapshot of the less illustrious side of Victorian times, allowing the reader to dip in and out and learn some of its more scandalous history. This period in history is rich with stories of the fascinating men and women who shaped it. *Not So Virtuous Victorians* serves up just a few of them for your consideration.

Child Labour

Rapid industrialisation led to a huge demand for labourers – both adult and children. It meant that children in the Victorian age worked in a vast range of roles, from chimney sweeps, domestic servants, coal miners, farm workers and rat catchers, to pickpockets and prostitutes.

The issue of poor industrial working conditions was prevalent; children were the easy option to hire simply because they were cheaper. They were also replaceable – the busy orphanages provided an ever-ready supply of young workers and due to their small size, children were given the unenviable task of crawling under machinery in textile mills to undertake repairs or opening and closing the ventilation doors in coal mines.

With steam effectively powering the Victorian age, coal mines were a huge part of industry. The constant darkness underground put a tremendous strain on the eyes, while the thick coal dust led to sight and respiratory problems. Match factories were another dubious source of employment; children were paid to dip the sticks into phosphorous and the chemical got into their lungs and rotted their teeth.

Annie Besant (1847 – 1933)

The case of The Queen v Charles Bradlaugh and Annie Besant scandalised Victorian society and turned Annie Besant into a household name.

Annie had started off doing everything right according to the standards of Victorian society. Born Annie Wood, she married clergyman Frank Besant at the age of 20. She wrote articles to supplement their marital income, but all that she earned was collected by her husband.

However, it wasn't too long before politics and disagreements

Annie Besant. (*Wellcome Library Digital Resources*)

about society caused friction in the marriage. Annie became increasingly disillusioned with religion altogether, eventually to Frank's consternation, refusing to attend communion. She came out in support of rights for farmworkers while Frank supported the landowners. Matters came to a head with their legal separation in 1873.

Annie fell in with a more socialist crowd, joining the National Secular Society and giving public speeches on free thought. She became close friends with atheist Charles Bradlaugh and the two edited *The National Reformer*, a weekly newspaper with features on progressive topics such as women's rights, trade unions and birth control.

Having set up their own publishing company, in 1877 Annie and Charles published *The Fruits of Philosophy*, which had been written by American writer Charles Knowlton, in 1832. It was about contraception and it caused outrage, especially within the Church. Frank must have been apoplectic. Anti-obscenity laws at the time forbade the distribution of any literary materials discussing reproduction and the two friends were arrested.

The subsequent trial lasted four days and although originally found guilty and sentenced to six months, they were freed upon appeal.

In 1888 Annie helped organise the strike by the female workers at the Bryant & May match factory in East London. She founded the Malthusian League, which promoted the use of contraception, and is remembered as a women's rights activist, social reformer and – having become involved in politics in India – a supporter of Indian nationalism.

Annie died in India on 20 September 1933, at the age of 85.

Match Girls

Match girls were young – some as young as 12 – and made matches by dipping the end of match sticks into toxic phosphorus. Many were poor Irish immigrants.

It was Annie Besant who investigated the Bryant & May Bow Road factory – the largest matchstick manufacturer in the country. What she saw left her appalled and she exposed their working conditions in an article on 23 June 1888, called 'White Slavery in London' in the publication *The Link*. She described it is a 'prison-house' and the female workers as 'undersized':

> Who cares for the fate of these white wage slaves? Born
> in slums, driven to work while still children, undersized

Advert for Bryant & May matches, which employed child labour. (*Wikiwand.com*) because underfed, oppressed because helpless, flung aside as soon as worked out, who cares if they die or go on the streets, provided only that the Bryant and May shareholders get their 23 per cent, and Mr. Theodore Bryant can erect statues and buy parks?

The factory owners, who had no legal obligation to safeguard their employees, were furious, dismissing the article as the 'twaddle of Mrs Besant and other socialists'. They attempted to force the hand of their employees, by strong-arming them into signing a document claiming they were very happy with their conditions.

The women refused. They were sick of working up to fourteen hours a day, (6.30 am to 6.00 pm, with just two breaks), the abysmal pay, huge fines simply for being late and related ill-health from exposure to deadly chemical fumes, including phossy jaw (phosphorous necrosis of the jaw) where the white phosphorus vapour destroyed and rotted the jaw bones. Phossy jaw could spread to the brain and unless the jaw was removed, it could lead to a horrifically painful death, as explained by bioarchaeologist Kristina Killgrove:

> People who were exposed in matchstick factories to white phosphorus are known historically to have developed physical ailments. Inhalation of phosphorus fumes could cause inflammation of the lungs and other pulmonary problems. Phosphorus hanging in the air and settling on walls and floors often gave the factory a blue-green glow. Workers went home with clothes that practically glowed in the dark, and those who inhaled too much phosphorus could have fluorescent vomit, bluish breath, and a glow around their mouths.

On 5 July 1888, 200 women walked out because three workers, accused by management of leaking information to Besant, were sacked. They marched towards Fleet Street, to the offices of *The Link*.

Women working in a match factory, possibly Bryant & May. (*Wikipedia*)

By the end of the day, 1,400 women had refused to work and ultimately wouldn't return for two weeks.

A strike fund was set up, with the support of Besant. Donations rolled in, many of the match girls went to Parliament to tell their stories, and the Union of Women Matchmakers (which became the largest female union in the country) was established.

It was a public relations disaster for the directors of Bryant & May who on Monday, 16 July, agreed to meet with the London Trades Council and the Match Girls Strike Committee. A deal was struck the next day, with terms that 'far exceeded the expectations', and the girls went back to work, triumphant, with improved working conditions, the provision of a breakfast room and the removal of all fines.

The Link reported that the strike had 'put new heart into all who are struggling for liberty and justice.' Nevertheless, it would be another two decades before it became illegal to use white phosphorus in match-making.

Sweeps

Children were worked extremely hard, with few or no breaks, and often in extremely dangerous environments. Chimney sweeps started

Young chimney sweep. (*funkidslive.com*)

from the age of 5, sometimes as young as 3, and were forced to clamber up into very narrow spaces. If they got stuck or scared, the sweep master would light a fire in the fireplace to 'encourage' them to move. If they weren't lucky enough to get themselves out, they suffocated. Scrabbling about in the dark scraped off layers of skin, which their bosses simply washed with salt water, and the inhalation of soot left many with lung damage. It wasn't unheard of for sweeps to be underfed by their sweep master to ensure they were thin enough to fit inside the chimneys.

By 1832 it was made illegal for children to sweep chimneys. The Chimney Sweepers and Chimneys Regulation Act of 1840 forbade anyone under the age of 21 from climbing into a chimney to clean it, voluntarily or otherwise. Nevertheless, child labour persisted. After the death of 12-year-old sweep George Brewster, who was killed while cleaning the chimney of Fulbourn Hospital in 1875, Lord Shaftesbury championed The Chimney Sweepers Act the same year, which proclaimed that all sweeps had to be registered with the police.

Other legislation during the Victorian age went some way to improving the lot of children, including the 1842 Mines Act, which made it illegal for boys under 10 and all women and girls, to work underground. The 1844 Factory Act restricted the working hours of both women and young people under the age of 18 to twelve on weekdays and nine on Saturdays; in 1847 the Ten Hour Act cut the hours of women and under-eighteens to ten a day and fifty-eight a week, and in 1850, it went further and set the working day for *all* workers at ten and a half hours.

Sex and Perversion

The Victorians are often perceived as being a self-flagellating, sexually frustrated, repressed, tight-arse lot.

There's no straight answer (no pun intended) to the question of Victorian attitudes towards sex. A lot of them are contradictory. Starting with the fact that Queen Victoria herself liked to draw and collect male nude figure drawings and even gave one to her husband as a present. Plus, the fact that Victoria and Albert themselves were first cousins, yet still married and had nine children. (That really is keeping it in the family.)

The image below shows Franz Xaver Winterhalter's painting *Florinda*, which Queen Victoria bought for Prince Albert's thirty-third birthday in 1852.

Florinda, 1853, by Franz Xaver Winterhalter. (*Royal Collection Trust*)

Writer Jan Marsh, who is an expert on the period says, 'According to their own testimonies, many people born in the Victorian age were both factually uninformed and emotionally frigid about sexual matters.'

As much as we have this puritanical, repressed side to the Victorian era, in direct contrast to the wild Regency period which preceded it, there was also a hidden lifestyle, which was much more liberated and featured pornography, perversion, prostitution, flogging and flagellation. Today, you'd describe families with a more censorious, conservative outlook as having 'Victorian' attitudes. But that might be doing our ancestors a huge disservice.

Masturbation and Erotica

Victorian women suffering from the one-size-fits-all malady of 'hysteria' (aka sexual frustration) were prescribed pelvic finger massage – and to alleviate the issue of stiff fingers, a 'massager' was invented; some Victorian women enjoyed the mechanical benefits of a 'lady's companion'.

Victorian physician and women's health advocate Clelia Duel Mosher researched and discussed the sexual behaviour of Victorian women, and included a study of the female orgasm:

> In addition to her research that proved women breathe from the diaphragm, just like men … that it was the corset and a lack of exercise that was to blame for many women's health issues. Her sexual survey work started in the 1890s and spanned 20 years, during which time she talked to 45 women at length about their sexual habits and preferences, from how often they had an orgasm to whether they experienced lust independent of their male partners.

The research revealed that some women took days to recover from the disappointment of not reaching orgasm; with one saying she experienced 'nerve-wracking-unbalancing if such conditions continue for any length of time', and another claiming that 'men have not been properly trained in this area.'

Queen Victoria, it should be noted, did not suffer from such sexual frustration; after her wedding night, she wrote in her private journal:

> It was a gratifying and bewildering experience. I never, never spent such an evening. His excessive love and affection gave me feelings of heavenly love and happiness. He clasped me in his arms and we kissed each other again and again.

Masturbation was frowned upon; indeed, it was seen as a sure cause of insanity. Referred to as self-pollution, self-abuse or onanism, disapproval of it gave rise to the development of the male anti-masturbation device (chastity belts for men).

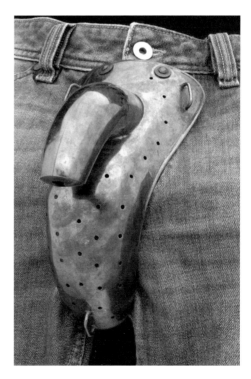

Part of male anti-masturbation device, late nineteenth or early twentieth century. (*Science Museum, London*)

Men were urged to practise sexual restraint in marriage, so as not to affect their intellectual prowess:

> 'That insanity arises from masturbation is now beyond a doubt,' declared one widely read authority, who also claimed that 'masturbators' became withdrawn, flabby, pale, self-mutilating and consumptive. Ailments afflicting adolescent girls were similarly said to signify abnormal sexual excitation. With punitive therapy in mind, some doctors erased sexual pleasure through barbaric practices such as penile cauterisation and clitoridectomy.

If you're reading this while eating your morning Kellogg's cornflakes, you may want to reconsider. The famous breakfast staple was originally invented to ward off masturbatory urges.

John Harvey Kellogg (1852 – 1943)

Writer Therese O'Neill says that Kellogg was the 'face of Victorian health, body and soul'. The American was obsessed with sexual abstinence, firmly believing that masturbation was the cause of many health problems from mood swings and bad posture to epilepsy and bad skin.

Married, but never consummating his union with his wife, Kellogg advocated a healthy diet as the best way to combat such desires. He said:

> Tea and coffee have led thousands to perdition in this way. Candies, spices, cinnamon, cloves, peppermint, and all strong essences, powerfully excite the genital organs and lead to the same result.

According to historian Fern Riddell, Kellogg believed a tasteless diet quelled sexual appetites, and decreed that mustard, pepper, rich gravy, beer, wine, cider and tobacco should all be avoided.

John Harvey Kellogg. (*Wikipedia*)

Kellogg was also anti-reading (for women anyway), in the belief that a voracious appetite for literature would, naturally, translate into an equally passionate appetite for masturbation and sexual urges. He said:

> Story books, romances, love tales, and religious novels constitute the chief part of the reading matter which American young ladies greedily devour. We have known

young ladies still in their teens who had read whole libraries of the most exciting novels … . The taste for novel-reading is like that for liquor or opium.

As for young boys, Kellogg advocated circumcision, without anaesthetic, for those with wandering hands. His view was that the discomfort following the procedure would be so intense, it would put boys off touching themselves. The fact that he also advocated the application of carbolic acid, as well as genital mutilation, literally puts us off our breakfast cereal for the foreseeable future. He added that:

the application of blisters [carbolic acid] and other irritants to the sensitive parts of the sexual organs, the removal of the clitoris and nymphaea, [labia minora] constitute the most proper treatment.

Pornography

The Pearl, A Magazine of Facetiae and Voluptuous Reading was a short-lived pornographic magazine that ran monthly for eighteen volumes (from July 1879 to December 1880), and had two Christmas specials until it was shot down in scandalised flames by the authorities for publishing obscenities.

Published by William Lazenby, an English pornographer of the 1870s and 1880s, *The Pearl* featured excerpts from three serialised stories per issue, as well as erotic parodies, vulgar poems (limericks appear frequently), and obscene short tales.

It holds the dubious distinction of featuring the first-known pornographic story based on American slavery and it's widely believed that many of the poems were actually written by Algernon Charles Swinburne, Victorian novelist, poet and six-time nominee for the Nobel Prize in Literature.

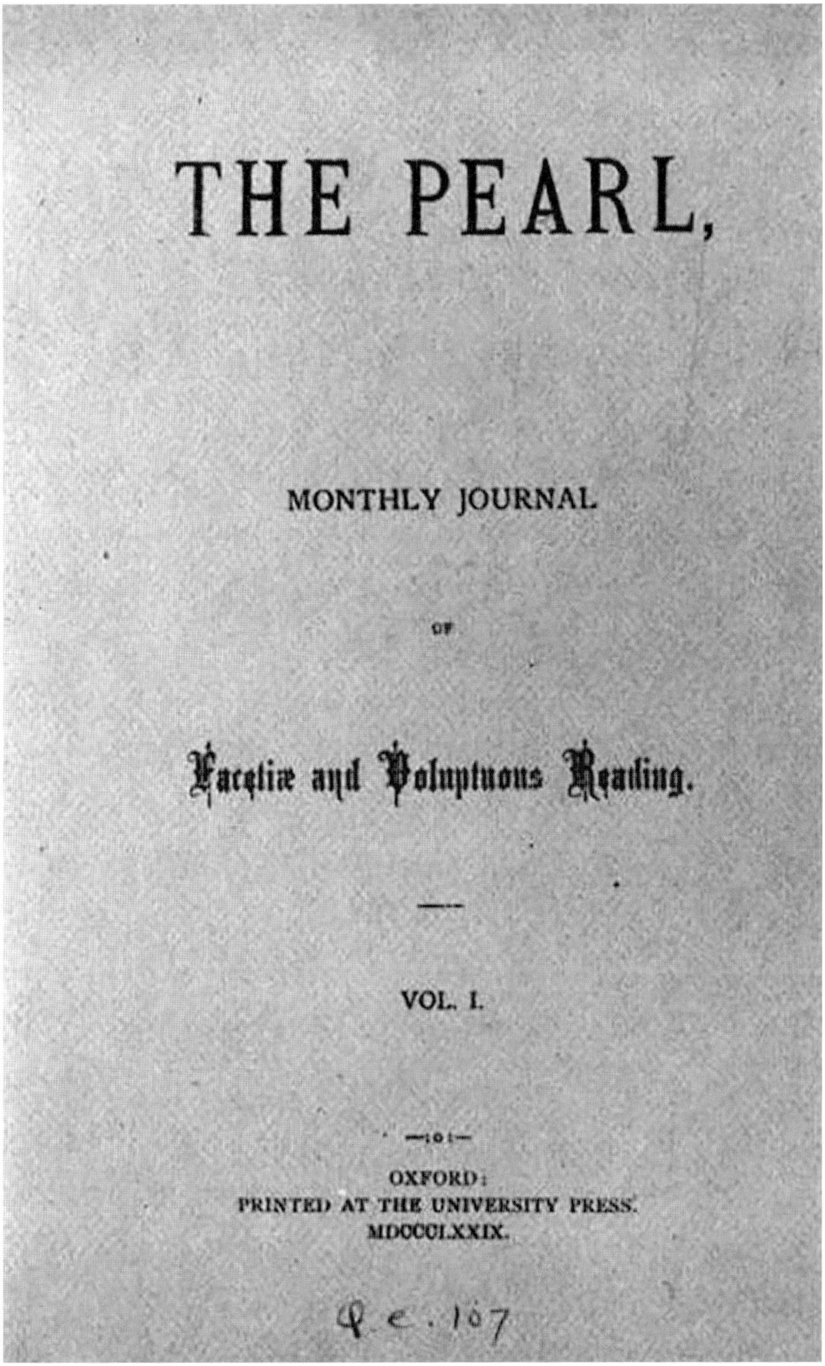

THE PEARL,

MONTHLY JOURNAL

OF

Facetiæ and Voluptuous Reading.

——

VOL. I.

—:o:—

OXFORD:
PRINTED AT THE UNIVERSITY PRESS.
MDCCCLXXIX.

The Pearl, June 1879. (*Wikipedia*)

Algernon Charles Swinburne, who was thought to have been the author of vulgar poems for pornographic magazine *The Pearl*. (*Wikipedia*)

The Whippingham Papers, a curious collection of stories and verse on flagellation, also included a number of unsigned works by Swinburne. Readers would no doubt have been whipped into a frenzy of delight with stories such as 'Arthur's Flogging', 'Miss Tickletouch', 'A Visit to Mrs Birch' and 'Young Ladies of the Academy'.

Swinburne, an Eton and Oxford alumnus, is described as a sadomasochist, obsessed with lesbianism and the Middle Ages. An alcoholic, he was a contemporary of Dante Gabriel Rossetti and William Morris.

Oscar Wilde said Swinburne was 'a braggart in matters of vice, who had done everything he could to convince his fellow citizens of his homosexuality and bestiality without being in the slightest degree a homosexual or a bestialiser.'

Also published by William Lazenby (with an initial print run of 250) was *The Sins of the Cities of the Plain or The Recollections of a Mary-Ann, with Short Essays on Sodomy and Tribadism*. It has been described as the 'one of the first exclusively homosexual pieces of English-language pornographic literature ever published'.

Other erotica examples include *Lady Pokingham* or *They all Do It*, and *The Wanton Lass*, where explicit descriptions of a lover's 'lordly priapus' flow seamlessly alongside elegiac depictions of the *mons veneris*, bawdy comments about 'keys in a man's pocket', whippings with a 'good birch rod', sexual awakenings, dirty jokes, limericks, songs and poems. For the curious amongst you they are still available online.

Then there are *The Nunnery Tales*, or *Cruising Under False Colours*, a sexual romp involving the Church, regarded as a classic of Victorian erotica. First published in Holland in the 1890s, it is thought to have been written (unsurprisingly by Anonymous) in 1866.

Fifty Shades of Grey enthusiasts looking to the origins of masochism will find them with Ritter von Leopold Sacher-Masoch's novella *Venus in Furs* in 1870 (which has been adapted into numerous films, most recently directed by Roman Polanski in 2013).

Christian Grey would have no doubt approved of that Victorian erotica and discipline classic *The Mysteries of Verbena House* or *Miss Bellasis Birched for Thieving*, which detailed the naughty exploits of students at a girls' boarding school and their subsequent stern punishments. It seems that the abundance of whipping and caning at British schools led many Victorian gentlemen, who were suffering withdrawal symptoms from the punishment, to frequent 'flagellation brothels' for a spot of submission.

Mary Jeffries ran the most exclusive and scandalous brothels of the time. Her chief assistant was a Mrs Travers, who kidnapped children by offering to watch them at stations while their parents went to gather luggage or buy tickets. Jeffries catered to the London elite and nobility and, chillingly, 'There was no form of sexual vice for which this murderess did not cater.'

Crusading journalist and Victorian social reformer W. T. Stead (1849 – 1912), writing for *The Pall Mall Gazette*, describes one of her houses:

> Flogging or birching goes on in brothels to a much greater degree than is generally believed. One of Mrs. Jeffries' rooms was fitted up like a torture chamber … . There were rings in the ceiling for hanging women and children up by the wrists, ladders for strapping them down at any angle, as well as the ordinary stretcher to which the victim is fastened so as to be unable to move. The instruments of flagellation included the ordinary birch, whips, holly branches and wire-thonged cat-o'-nine-tails.

There's also mention of the practice of 'figging', which to those with a 'burning' interest (the clue is in the description) involved a finger-sized amount of ginger and your rectum.

The Victorians were actually extremely interested in sex. 'They had a prurient fascination with all things sexual – scandals, adultery, homosexual liaisons,' says Dr Anne Hanley, lecturer at Birkbeck, University of London and consultant on the series *Victoria*, 'and lapped it up in a press which condemned them with one breath and titillated with another.'

Syphilis

When it wasn't only the upper lip that was stiff, there was some practical sense in urging the sexually adventurous to curb their voracious appetite: the venereal disease syphilis was rife. 'Stigmatising infections, lengthy treatments and uncertain outcomes took an emotional toll on patients,' adds Hanley. 'Nineteenth-century doctors took seriously the notion that a diagnosis of syphilis could trigger acute despair and melancholia.'

Syphilis knew no distinction in class or rank; wives and children alike became infected. Considerable social stigma accompanied the disease and it was not well understood, with many susceptible people unaware of its existence. 'In the prudish Victorian imagination, syphilis was inextricable from the other great "social evil", prostitution, and represented physical and moral decay,' adds Hanley.

Unsurprisingly, it was the men who were most protected, their wives often in complete ignorance. Having knowledge of syphilis was considered disgraceful – it symbolised that a woman who knew about it was impure. In fact, 'concealment was so common as to become the subject of fraught medical and social debate.' And those rich men who caught the disease from brothels or prostitutes were given considerably more sympathy than the 'working girls' who'd had to resort to the world's oldest profession to earn a living. Women, explains Hanley, were often unaware of the cause of their malaise:

> If a husband infected his wife with syphilis or gonorrhoea, a doctor went to great lengths, usually at the behest of the husband, to conceal the cause of her illness. She would know that she was ill, but she wouldn't necessarily know that she had VD. Doctors who withheld information from women claimed that they were bound by patient confidentiality – a doctor couldn't tell a wife that she was suffering from syphilis because doing so would reveal

that her husband also had syphilis. A degree of pragmatic paternalism informed these decisions: doctors believed that they knew best and prioritised expediency. After all, a woman who discovered that she was infected with VD might cause a fuss and make her husband's life difficult. And since the husband was usually the one paying the doctor's fee, his interests took priority.

And the inequality in the knowledge of the disease also extended to the treatment. She adds:

> Before socialised healthcare, the quality of your treatment largely depended on your class and income. Charitable hospitals like St Bartholomew's that cared for the urban poor eventually refused to treat VD patients. Wholly reliant upon charitable donation, they were beholden to their benefactors, many of whom still viewed syphilis and gonorrhoea as punishment for vice. Consequently, the treatment of the poor was determined by the prejudices and moral sensibilities of the wealthy.

Prostitution and the Fallen Woman

Victorian society called prostitution the 'great social evil'. Women 'fell' into prostitution for a variety of social and economic reasons – their downfall was into a life devoid of purity, chastity and grace. So for many it may have been viewed as a 'great social evil', but for those struggling to get by, it was simply a way to make a living.

It's important to clarify that the word 'prostitute' encompassed a range of situations that women found themselves in – it wasn't just for those who sold their bodies for sex. It would also refer to women who were living with men outside marriage, or women who had had

'The Great Social Evil', John Leech, Punch, 10 January 1857. (*Victorianweb.org*)

illegitimate children, or perhaps had relations with men for pleasure rather than money.

In 1791, a police officer estimated that there were 50,000 prostitutes in London, but at least half this figure consisted of unmarried women living with a partner, while only 20,000 referred to what we would today call prostitutes.

There could have been as many as 80,000 prostitutes working in Victorian London. Gender historian Lisa Nolland suggests that women working as factory workers, servants and seamstresses were those most likely to become 'fallen women':

> Women who worked in factories worked alongside men for long hours and sometimes late into the night; this type of setting often led to cases of corruption and rape. Women who worked as seamstresses had an entirely different set of problems that led to prostitution. Although they were not exposed to men as those in factories were, they were over-worked and underpaid. There were many seamstresses, but there was not enough work for all of them; therefore, many women who were rooted in this profession used prostitution as a supplementary income in order to avoid starvation. Finally, women who worked as servants in the households of the middle and/or upper classes were often forced into prostitution. Oftentimes, they were either seduced or forced into a sexual liaison by their bosses. Because of the inequality in their professional relationship and social status, these women did not have the choice of saying, 'no', and once their virtue was lost, any prospect of a future marriage was also lost.

Unsurprisingly, the government's main concern when it came to controlling prostitution, which resulted in many cases of VD, was not the health of the women, but that of the military men they engaged with. It was for the safety of the Armed Forces that they passed The Contagious Diseases Acts of 1864, 1866 and 1869. These laws gave officials the 'unquestionable' right to a form of citizen's arrest of any woman living in a military town or seaport that they believed was a prostitute and carrying a disease, in order to submit them, forcefully, to a medical examination.

One can imagine the abuses of power this would have created and the number of working women mistaken for prostitutes and forced to endure not just the humiliation and trauma of being detained, but the intrusive medical examination that followed.

For women who were making a living as prostitutes, there were a number of ways they could peddle their wares. Judith Walkowitz, Professor of History at Johns Hopkins University and author of *Prostitution and Victorian Society*, says the most common form of prostitution was streetwalking, which was used primarily by women supplementing their daily income, although some relied on it as a primary source. Adds Walkowitz: 'There were many dangers in this avenue of employment. Women who worked the streets were often subjected to poverty, insecurity, physical danger, alcoholism, disease and police harassment.'

She adds that a safer way to work would be in a brothel or by targeting the transient military customers:

> This does not mean that prostitutes who worked in alternate avenues, such as the encampments of soldiers or brothels, did not experience many of the same difficulties, but these dangers were normally less severe. Prostitutes that followed the encampments of soldiers or worked the ports of sailors were normally provided for on a night-by-night basis depending on the man they would next sleep with. These women enjoyed a certain amount of security in the knowledge that women were few and far between

in such areas and, therefore, they were somewhat valued for their attributes. Those prostitutes that worked in brothels were also ordinarily provided a certain level of security under the brothel-owner. During the Victorian Age, the number of prostitutes who actually lived in brothels was considerably low. Despite this, customers that behaved inappropriately towards the prostitutes that did inhabit such places were normally unappreciated and unwelcome.

W. T. Stead, crusading journalist, Victorian social reformer and pioneer of investigative reporting, uncovered the white slave trade in Britain by proving that he could purchase a 13-year-old girl in London for sex.

Going undercover in Charles Street (today's Ranston Street) in Lisson Grove, near Marylebone, he bought 13-year-old Eliza Armstrong from her mother, for £5, ostensibly for domestic service. With a former prostitute as the 'middleman', the sting went ahead and Stead agreed to meet Armstrong at a brothel in Poland Street.

He detailed his findings in a series of three highly controversial evening edition articles in *The Pall Mall Gazette* from 6-10 July 1885 called 'The Maiden Tribute of Modern Babylon'. They caused an absolute uproar. Here is an extract of Stead interviewing a police officer familiar with the racket:

> 'But,' I continued, 'are these maids willing or unwilling parties to the transaction – that is, are they really maiden, not merely in being each a *virgo intacta* in the physical sense, but as being chaste girls who are not consenting parties to their seduction?'
>
> He looked surprised at my question, and then replied emphatically: 'Of course they are rarely willing, and as a rule they do not know what they are coming for.'

Journalist W. T. Stead, who went to prison after proving he could buy a child for sex.

'But,' I said in amazement, 'then do you mean to tell me that in very truth actual rapes, in the legal sense of the word, are constantly being perpetrated in London on unwilling virgins, purveyed and procured to rich men at so much a head by keepers of brothels?'

'Certainly,' said he, 'there is not a doubt of it.'

'Why,' I exclaimed, 'the very thought is enough to raise hell.'

'It is true,' he said, 'and although it ought to raise hell, it does not even raise the neighbours.'

'But do the girls cry out?'

'Of course they do. But what avails screaming in a quiet bedroom? Remember, the utmost limit of howling or excessively violent screaming, such as a man or woman would make if actual murder was being attempted, is only two minutes, and the limit of screaming of any kind is only five ... . But suppose the screams continue and you get uneasy, you begin to think whether you should not do something? Before you have made up your mind and got dressed the screams cease, and you think you were a fool for your pains ... . Once a girl gets into such a house she is almost helpless and may be ravished with comparative safety.'

The articles focused on the sale, purchase and violation of children; the procuration of virgins; the entrapment and ruin of women; the international slave trade in girls and atrocities, brutalities, and unnatural crimes. The exposé, later interpreted by George Bernard Shaw in his 1912 play *Pygmalion*, led to Stead's temporary imprisonment:

London was shocked by the details. The Gazette's offices in Northumberland Street were besieged by thousands seeking copies. In strident prose – 'the hour of democracy has come' – Stead justified his tactics, demanding that the legal age of consent be raised from 13 to 16. Stead had pushed back the envelope of acceptable British journalism and it came at an immediate price. Because he had gained Eliza's mother's permission only – rather than her father's as well – Stead had broken the law as it then stood. Along with five others he was arrested for kidnapping. Convicted at the Old Bailey in October – for the same crime he had exposed – Stead was imprisoned for three months in Holloway Prison.

This was despite the fact his investigation led to the Criminal Law Amendment Act of 1885, which did raise the age of consent from 13 to 16 and increased the strength of the current laws against prostitution. However, it also re-criminalised homosexual acts.

Stead was among the 1,500 people who perished on the *Titanic* on 15 April 1912.

Jack the Ripper

One of the world's most famous serial killers – his name still sends a chill down the spine – remains one of England's most notorious unsolved crimes and has spawned an entire industry around books (at least 100), walking tours, tourism and TV spin-offs. Jack the Ripper has been good for business.

Between August and November 1888, he murdered at least five women in the Whitechapel district in London's East End (while he was thought to have killed many more, these women, known as the 'canonical five' are singled out as being the work of one person). Contrary to the mythology that has grown around his victims, only two of the women (Elizabeth Stride and Mary Jane Kelly) were sex workers. According to Hallie Rubenhold, historian and writer of *The Five: The Untold Lives of the Women Killed by Jack the*

Ripper, the five women were murdered while sleeping rough on the streets:

> The more I looked for evidence of sex work, the more I found that it just simply wasn't there. What I found instead was a lot of convoluted, confused definition of what prostitution was among the working classes

'The Ripper', from The Illustrated Police News. (*The British Library Board*)

and the poor. It is all bound up with sexual practices, partnerships, sex outside of marriage, how people lived with each other – all totally at odds with what we call 'Victorian morality'. [That morality was determined] by the dominant upper class, not the majority working class. We have a cognitive bias – this lack of evidence has been conveniently overlooked, because it isn't part of the accepted story.

Four of the five working-class women were in their forties. Mary Jane Kelly, the exception, was around 25 years old.

Rubenhold goes on to challenge the historical legacy of the women:

Instead of a shared profession, what the five had in common was tragedy. It is striking, when reading their stories, how easy it is to understand why they fled their homes, why they turned to drink. Polly enjoyed a short-lived step up the social ladder when she moved into Peabody housing with her family, then endured the indignity of watching her husband fall in love with a younger neighbour. Six of Annie's eight children were born – some living only briefly – with some physical impact from her alcoholism, which would also cause her husband to throw her out of their Knightsbridge home. Catherine was an orphan and vagrant, taking her two children with her to the workhouse or prison, away from her physically abusive husband; a third baby starved in her arms.

Rubenhold believes Mary Jane narrowly escaped being trafficked to mainland Europe – she returned hastily from a trip to Paris – a common experience among sex workers at the time. And as a young maid in Sweden, Elizabeth was placed on a 'register of shame'. She was unmarried and pregnant – probably by her employer – and so suspected of being a sex worker. Her new status left her unable to get any work other than on the streets. The last years of her life in London were peppered with drunken, angry incidents that Rubenhold suggests could have been the first signs of neurosyphilis, disguised by heavy drinking. 'Her desire to numb herself and rage at the world,' believes Rubenhold 'was a natural one'.

These victims, all discovered with their throats cut and bodies mutilated in a manner suggesting surgical or anatomical experience, were:

Mary Ann 'Polly' Nicholls (found 31 August)

Annie Chapman (found 8 September)

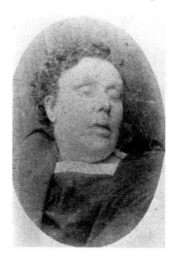

Elizabeth Stride (found 30 September)

Catherine Eddowes (found 30 September)

Mary Jane Kelly (found 9 November)

To this day, theories abound as to the Ripper's identity, which has never been confirmed. It's thought that the murders, which took place within a mile of each other, stopped because the police came close to identifying him. The public fury over their inability to catch him led to the resignations of the Home Secretary and London's Police Commissioner.

The cover of the 21 September 1889 issue of *Puck* magazine featuring cartoonist Tom Merry's depiction of the unidentified Whitechapel murderer Jack the Ripper.

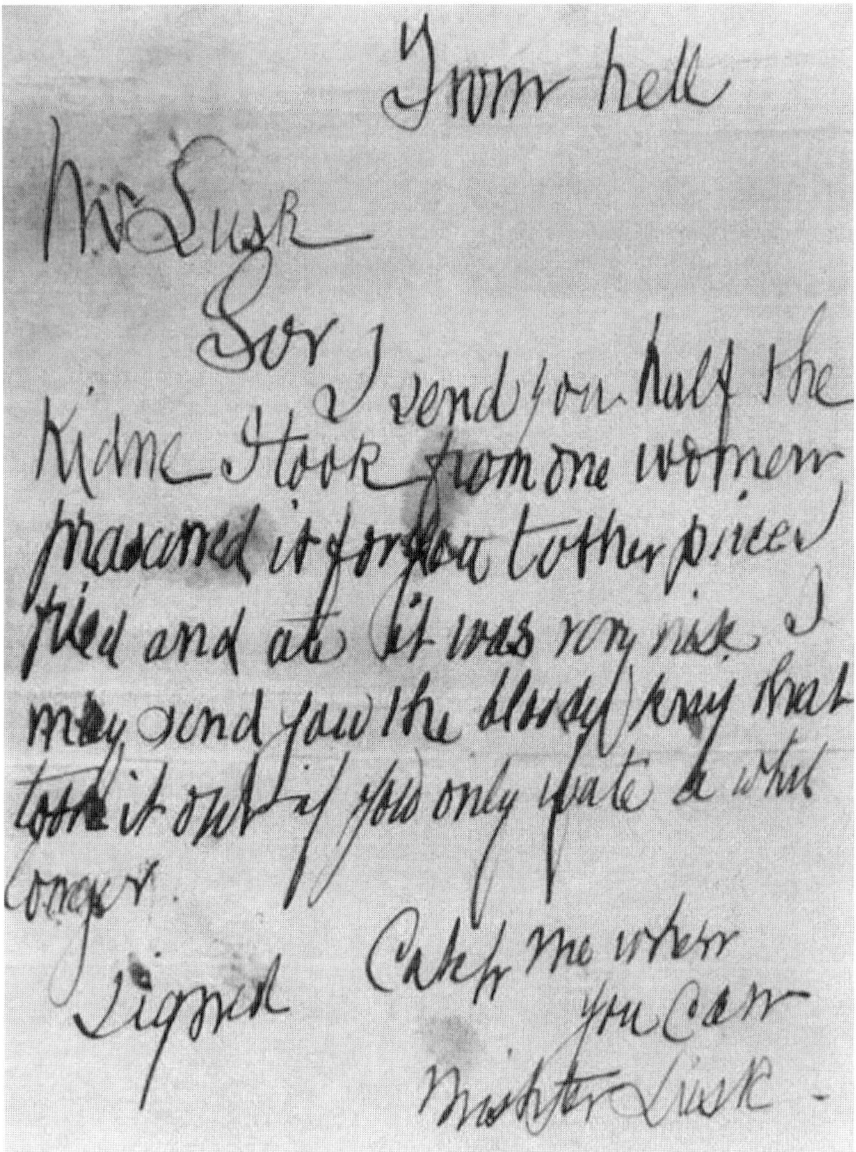

From hell

Mr Lusk

Sor I send you half the
Kidne I took from one women
prasarved it for you tother piece I
fried and ate it was very nise I
may send you the bloody knif that
took it out if you only wate a whil
longer

Signed   Catch me when
                    you can
            Mishter Lusk -

Hundreds of letters purporting to be from the murderer were sent to Scotland Yard; most were dismissed as fakes but three were thought to be genuine. These are the 'Dear Boss' letter, (which first used the moniker 'Jack the Ripper'; the 'Saucy Jacky' postcard and the 'From Hell' letter.

Dear Boss,

I keep on hearing the police have caught me but they wont fix me just yet. I have laughed when they look so clever and talk about being on the right track. That joke about Leather Apron gave me real fits *[prostitutes claimed they saw a mysterious character wearing a leather apron]. I am down on whores and I shant quit ripping them till I do get buckled. Grand work the last job was. I gave the lady no time to squeal. How can they catch me now. I love my work and want to start again. You will soon hear of me with my funny little games. I saved some of the proper red stuff in a ginger beer bottle over the last job to write with but it went thick like glue and I cant use it. Red ink is fit enough I hope ha. ha. The next job I do I shall clip the ladys ears off and send to the police officers just for jolly wouldn't you. Keep this letter back till I do a bit more work, then give it out straight. My knife's so nice and sharp I want to get to work right away if I get a chance. Good Luck.*

Yours truly
Jack the Ripper

Dont mind me giving the trade name

PS Wasnt good enough to post this before I got all the red ink off my hands curse it No luck yet. They say I'm a doctor now. ha ha [Rumours abounded that his crimes proved he must have had medical training.]

****

Saucy Jacky
I was not codding dear old Boss when I gave you the tip, you'll hear about Saucy Jacky's work tomorrow double

event this time number one squealed a bit couldn't finish straight off. ha not the time to get ears for police. thanks for keeping last letter back till I got to work again.

Jack the Ripper

The 'From Hell' letter was sent on 16 October, in a cardboard box, to George Lusk, president of the Whitechapel Vigilance Committee, together with half a human kidney, preserved in wine. Medical examination of the kidney found it to be similar (although findings were inconclusive) to that removed from Catherine Eddowes.

From hell.
Mr Lusk,
Sor
I send you half the Kidne I took from one woman and prasarved it for you tother piece I fried and ate it was very nise. I may send you the bloody knif that took it out if you only wate a whil longer

signed
Catch me when you can Mishter Lusk

In addition to numerous conspiracy theories around cults and the police covering up the case because 'Jack' was in fact a member of high society or even from the royal family, the main suspects were:

Montague Druitt: a barrister and teacher with an interest in surgery who was said to be insane. He disappeared after the final murders and was later found dead, apparently from suicide.

Michael Ostrog, a Russian thief and conman who had been placed in an asylum because of his homicidal tendencies.

George Chapman, originally from Poland, where he apprenticed for a surgeon, trained in surgery and worked as a nurse. Despite having a wife at home, he married a young Polish girl when he moved to London in 1888. During an argument with his first wife, he calmly told her exactly how he could kill her and dispose of her body. The marriage didn't last. He continued to womanise, using liaisons with mistresses (and a third wife) to obtain money and their inheritances, then beat them and poisoned them. He was eventually found guilty of the murder of his previous wives, who all died from poisoning by tartar-emetic, similar to arsenic. He was hanged on 7 April 1903.

Aaron Kosminski, a 23-year-old Polish Jew, professional barber and resident of Whitechapel who was known to hate women (particularly sex workers) and who was hospitalised in an asylum several months after the last murder. There were no further Ripper murders after his incarceration. He died in 1919 at the age of 53.

Several notable Londoners of the era, such as the painter Walter Sickert and the physician Sir William Gull, have also been subjects of such speculation.

Hidden Sexualities

Historian Jeff Evans worked his way through more than a quarter of a million criminal records at the National Archive at Kew, from the 1850s to the 1960s. He discovered that the Victorians were actually more lenient towards homosexuality than the liberal generation from the so-called Swinging Sixties.

Dracula author Bram Stoker

As for the love that dare not speak its name – sapphic or lesbian relationships, the Victorians didn't so much as turn a blind eye as close them altogether.

Homosexual acts were a capital offence until 1861, and in 1885 gay sex behind closed doors was made a criminal offence. Literary icon Oscar Wilde would be imprisoned in 1896. Lesbian and sapphic sex were due to be criminalised in the 1885 law until Queen Victoria herself declared them to be impossible; and if she said lesbians didn't exist, how could the rest of her country argue with her?

The author of *Dracula*, Bram Stoker was himself in the closet. He was a repressed homosexual as well as a good friend of Oscar Wilde. On the topic of Wilde, a profile of Victorian sexuality wouldn't be complete without his story.

Oscar Wilde (1854 – 1900)

Irish playwright, novelist, superb wit and poet, Wilde's status as a literary genius, dandy and icon of the era is often overshadowed by the scandal of his personal life and hidden homosexuality. He had kept his sexuality a secret, marrying children's writer Constance Lloyd on 29 May 1884 and having two sons.

He used his writing to satirise the hypocrisy of Victorian ideals: its society, morality, aristocracy, class distinctions and views on marriage, most notably through the play *The Importance of Being Earnest*, (first performed in 1895) where he exposed the double standards of the Victorian aristocracy and the differences between the 'proper' behaviour and identities they displayed in public and the less salubrious ones effected in private.

Wilde began an affair with Lord Alfred Douglas, aka Bosie, the son of the Marquis of Queensberry, and sixteen years his junior, in 1891.

The marquis was horrified at the relationship and attempted to expose Wilde, leaving a homophobic calling card for him at the private London club, the Albemarle, which read 'For Oscar Wilde, posing somdomite' [*sic*].

Playwright and homosexual, Oscar Wilde.

With homosexual acts a criminal offence in England (they remained illegal until 1967), Wilde had no option but to fight for his reputation. He took the marquis to court at the Old Bailey for libel on 3 April 1895.

However, the trial worked against Wilde, with his private life being put on display for all to see, as male prostitutes he'd engaged with were called as witnesses.

Margaret Cotta, a chambermaid at The Savoy Hotel, described the scene she encountered after a visit by Wilde and Bosie. She had 'found a common boy, rough looking, about 14 years of age' in Wilde's bed, the sheets of which 'were always in a most disgusting state ... [with] traces of vaseline, soil and semen.'

Wilde was arrested and put on trial for gross indecency with men.

The court transcriptions are a testament to Wilde's courage and unfailing, unflappable wit. In the reading of letters between Wilde and Bosie, it was in the courtroom that the chilling and resonant euphemism for homosexuality, the 'love that dare not speak its name', was coined. When questioned about its meaning, Wilde said: 'It is that deep spiritual affection that is as pure as it is perfect. It dictates and pervades great works of art … . It is beautiful, it is fine, it is the noblest form of affection … . The world mocks at it, and sometimes puts one in the pillory for it.'

He was convicted and sentenced to two years' hard labour. The experience destroyed his health and Wilde died on 30 November 1900, at the age of 46. He was buried in Paris.

Scandal of 19 Cleveland Street

Towards the latter end of Victoria's reign, police discovered young telegraph boys working at a homosexual brothel in the heart of London's Fitzrovia.

On 4 July 1889, 15-year-old telegraph boy Charles Swinscow was searched by police as they investigated stolen money at his place of work, the General Post Office. His earnings should have been around eleven shillings, but the police found eighteen shillings in his pockets and took him in for questioning.

It didn't take long for Charles to break under pressure. He confessed that he was working for Charles Hammond at a house in Cleveland Street; for four shillings a time, he allowed the brothel's clients to 'have a go between my legs' and 'put their persons into me'. He also gave up the names of several other telegraph boys who were involved.

As Oscar Wilde would discover to his social detriment only a few years later in 1895, sexual acts between men were illegal at the time. The officer in charge of the investigation was Frederick Abberline, who had been involved in the Jack the Ripper case in 1888. Despite being determined to arrest Hammond on charges of conspiracy 'to commit the abominable crime of buggery', Hammond fled abroad before he could be prosecuted.

There was talk of the government scurrying to cover up the incident to protect the identities of several high-ranking aristocrats including Henry Fitzroy, Earl of Euston, and other VIPs, some allegedly linked to the royal family.

Anne Lister of Shibden (1791 – 1840)

'I love, and only love, the fairer sex'

Also known as Britain's first 'modern lesbian', with writings dubbed the 'Rosetta Stone of lesbian history', Anne Lister was a wealthy Victorian landowner known to locals as 'Gentleman Jack'. A great intellectual with a passionate interest in science, she once dissected a woman's head during a private anatomy lesson in Paris.

Born in Halifax, West Yorkshire, she was the daughter of an army captain who fought in the American War of Independence and a Yorkshire woman from Welton. She had four brothers (three of whom died young, and a fourth, Jeremy, who drowned in 1813) and a sister, Marian. With Jeremy's death, she became heir presumptive to the

The corrected plaque honouring Anne Lister, Holy Trinity Church, York. It originally described her as 'gender non-conforming'.

400 acre Shibden Hall Estate, which had been in the family for two centuries.

She was way ahead of her time as a woman determined to live her life as she wanted. And her fortune and property enabled her to do so. A smart businesswoman, she expanded Shibden's collieries, outmanoeuvring, out-smarting and out-negotiating other men in the industry. She referred to traditional marriage as legalised prostitution.

The twenty-four volumes (around four million words) of *Diaries and Journals of Mrs Lister of Shibden Hall in Halifax, Yorkshire* were two exercise books and twenty-four hardback volumes written largely in a

Shibden Hall, Halifax.

secretive code, which was broken by the son of her distant cousin, John Lister (who had inherited the house), and Arthur Burrell, in the 1890s.

Initially, John and Arthur were shocked by the salacious and sexually scandalous content of the journals, and Arthur urged John to burn them. John also wanted to destroy the evidence, probably because any publicity might draw attention to his own alleged homosexuality, which was punishable by law.

Luckily for us, John instead, chose to hide them behind wood panelling; they would be rediscovered after his death in 1933, when Shibden Hall was transformed into a museum for the people of Halifax.

Helena Whitbread, editor and decoder of the modern version of the diaries, says:

> The idea of using an esoteric code appears to have had
> its roots in Anne's burgeoning knowledge of the Greek
> language: she mingles Greek letters with other symbols

of her own devising. She felt safe in the belief that no one would be able to decipher the coded passages, and as her confidence grew, they became longer and much more explicit when dealing with those aspects of her life which could not be written about in 'plainhand'.

What they discovered, in the words of Arthur Burrell, was 'an intimate account of homosexual practices among Miss Lister and her many "friends"; hardly any one of them escaped her.'

Whitbread describes Lister as a sexual pioneer. She says:

> The history of the sexual life of Anne Lister remained behind an iron curtain of conspiracy by those 'in the know' – a handful of Halifax town officials and one or two scholars. That situation was about to change. The liberalising decade of the 1960s saw the introduction of the Sexual Offences Act (1967), which legalised homosexual activity so long as it was conducted in private and between consenting adults. The following two decades saw an extension of this climate of toleration and, as the homosexual community became more visible and vocal in their demand for equal rights, it became possible to speak, or write, openly about the lives of lesbian or gay people.

Historian Emma Donoghue has described the Lister diaries as 'the Dead Sea Scroll' of lesbian history. Ellie Cawthorne, writing for *BBC History Magazine* says: 'Anne Lister's journals are densely packed with the minutiae of her everyday life. Yet buried between exhaustive entries on the political situation in Prussia, canal tolls and toenail cutting are extraordinary accounts of her romantic and sexual adventures with women.'

Lister earned the name 'Gentleman Jack' from the male residents of Halifax who took umbrage at her taking on a 'male' role in her industrial undertakings, and because she dressed like a man and wore black clothes, black boots and a top hat. She also owned property, had shares in canal and railway businesses and owned a coal mine.

She disliked being seen as a woman, admitting to having 'sensitiveness of anything that reminded me of my petticoats' and wrote in her journals that she wore gentleman's breeches to hold up her underwear. 'Yet my manners are certainly peculiar, not all masculine but rather softly gentleman-like. I know how to please this fair maiden of mine,' she wrote.

She accentuated her masculine attributes and did nothing to hide her lesbianism, with essayist Rictor Norton saying, 'Her flirting with women is so open and gentleman-like that several women of her acquaintance wonder if she is a man in disguise. She is aware that her sexuality is an object of discussion among friends and relatives.'

'The people generally remark, as I pass along, how much I am like a man,' wrote Anne in her journal. Labelled a tomboy from a young age, she was alienated at boarding school, which she was sent to by her exasperated mother. There, she confided in her diary, as noted many years later by bbc.co.uk:

> So obsessive was her personality, no detail was left out: the time she woke up and how long she'd slept; the letters she received and their contents; the day's weather; the time it took to walk into town; whether she'd enjoyed veal cutlets or mutton for dinner. Everything she had learned that day would be recorded too: Greek, algebra, French, mathematics, geology, astronomy and philosophy. Anne possessed a voracious intelligence and – at a time when women were barred from universities – was determined to learn everything a man was able to.

Her first sexual encounter was with a fellow female pupil at the age of 15; Eliza Raine, similarly a social outcast due to her illegitimacy (the half-Indian daughter of an English doctor). She joined Anne in her living quarters in the attic rooms of Manor House School in York. Anne eventually tired of Eliza and moved onto greener pastures, but her young lover never recovered emotionally from the trauma and was sent to The Retreat, or Quakers' Asylum at Clifton, which was otherwise known as a lunatic asylum.

Anne was intrigued by her own 'oddity'. She trawled books on anatomy to comprehend where her feelings came from, but was unable to find anything as bbc.co.uk adds:

> But as she came to terms with her sexuality, there was no self-loathing. Her feelings were entirely natural, she believed: her God-given right. Women, while usually confused about their feelings for Anne, were typically captivated by her. Anne was promiscuous and arguably predatory, moving efficiently from one lover to the next, without them penetrating her heart.

'I love and only love the fairer sex and thus beloved by them in turn, my heart revolts from any love but theirs' wrote Anne in her diary on 29 October 1820.

The love of Anne's life was doctor's daughter Mariana Belcombe, who was 23 when they met. They kept in touch by travelling the 40 miles between their homes in York and Halifax by horse and cart, wrote letters and even exchanged rings in a commitment ceremony. Anne was devastated when, in 1815, aged 25, Mariana declared she was getting married to a 56-year-old widower, Charles Lawton. Even more painful for her, tradition held that the close female friend of the bride would accompany the newly-married happy couple on their honeymoon: this lot fell to Anne. Once returned home to Shibden, she confided in her journal, furiously accusing her former beloved of 'legal prostitution'.

Anne would continue her numerous love affairs (one of them with Mariana's older sister Anne), until reconnecting with Mariana a year later (apparently with Charles' consent). Their passionate affair continued in secret. Anne wrote:

> She herself suggested a kiss. I thought it dangerous and would have declined but she persisted. I took off my pelisse and drawers, got into bed and had a very good kiss, she showing all due inclination and in less than seven minutes, the door was unbolted and we were all right again.

A 'kiss' was Anne's code for sex, and writing that she had 'incurred a cross' referred to her experiencing an orgasm – X really did mark the spot. She also described sexual fulfilment with women as 'going to Italy', giving the oft-quoted rite of passage for cultured ladies of 'embarking on the European tour' a whole new meaning.

In September 1825, the two had a recommitment ceremony, exchanging lockets containing their own pubic hair (this was despite Anne contracting a sexually transmitted infection that Charles had given Mariana).

However, Anne's passionate declarations, intentions of acting as if Mariana were her wife and indiscretions made Mariana fearful they would be exposed to a scandalised society and she began to withdraw her affections, devastating Anne once again. 'Oh, women, women!' she wrote. 'I am always taken up with some girl or other. When shall I amend?'

Anne fled to Paris in 1824 to nurse her broken heart, which she did for eight months by engaging in further romantic and sexual escapades. She had a love of travel, visiting several countries over the next fifteen years and falling in and out of love, while attempting to climb the social ladder of society and improve her rank. When her friendship with beautiful Vere Hobart, sister of the Earl of Buckinghamshire, failed to transform into anything romantic, and Vere became engaged to an army officer, she despaired once more.

'My high society plans fail,' she wrote in her diaries. 'I have had my whim – tried the thing – & pretty much it has cost me. I have been an Icarus – but shall fall less fatally, for I can still live and be happy. Here I am at forty-one, with a heart to seek. What will be the end of it?'

She returned home to Halifax and on reacquainting herself with 29-year-old heiress Ann Walker, fell in love with her and her fortune, which she hoped would fulfil her ambitious plans for her estates and property as well as enable her to continue travelling abroad.

Anne wrote in her diary: 'She little dreams what is in my mind. She has money and this might make up for rank. We get on very well so far.' She went on to record the number of orgasms she had while thinking of Ann, and as the relationship progressed, those she experienced as they became intimate.

Anne being Anne was forthright in her desire to be married and live as a couple, but Ann was not so sure, leaving Ms Lister to decamp in a fury to Paris and Copenhagen. On her return, with Anne now

42, it seemed her lover was on the cusp of changing her mind. The couple changed their wills in favour of each other and Anne informed her family. The plan was for each woman to give the other a ring as a token of their commitment.

'Had she been a man, Lister's liaison with Ann Walker would have been seen as an ideal marriage, uniting properties and policies to form a powerful Tory gentry base at the edge to industrializing

Anne Lister, played by Suranne Jones, and Ann Walker, played by Sophie Rundle, in *Gentleman Jack*. (*Jay Brooks*)

Halifax,' wrote Martha Vicinus in *Intimate Friends: Women Who Loved Women, 1778–1928*.

They were 'married' on Easter Sunday 1834 at Holy Trinity Church in York. The act of taking communion together was all the ceremony Anne needed to feel it was official, and the happy couple enjoyed a three-month honeymoon travelling through France and Switzerland.

The scandal was the talk of Yorkshire. Two prominent women co-habiting as if they were husband and wife caused outrage: a mocking advert appeared in *The Leeds Mercury* announcing the marriage of 'Captain Tom Lister of Shibden Hall to Miss Ann Walker'. Anonymous letters also arrived addressed to 'Captain Lister' congratulating the couple 'on their happy connection'.

The marriage was far from plain sailing, with the two women being so different in character. Large amounts of money were sunk into renovating Shibden, and the couple embarked on further travels, including the Pyrenees, where Anne indulged her love of mountaineering. Eventually they reached Russia, where, on 11 August 1840, Anne died from a fever induced by an insect bite. She was 49. Her wife was left thousands of miles from home, and it took her eight months to return, alongside her wife's coffin. Anne was buried in Halifax Minster.

Ann inherited the estate, but the Walker family believed her to be mentally incapacitated and arranged for a break in by a doctor, policeman and lawyer (the holy trinity) at Shibden, where Ann was discovered crouched behind a locked door, surrounded by paperwork and a host of pistols. She was declared insane and dispatched to the same asylum where Eliza Raine still resided. She died in 1854 at the age of 51 and was buried in St Matthew's Church in Lightcliffe.

Despite Anne Lister's notoriety, which made her seem unique, and her legacy as the 'first modern lesbian', Caroline Gonda of Cambridge University is insistent that she was definitely 'not the only gay in the village.' Adds Gonda: 'Although Anne is a bit of a bad lass, a bedpost notcher, and a terrible snob, she tells us so much about sexual desire in lesbian history.'

Author and lesbian Jeanette Winterson says Lister was a role model to her, saying, 'To act like a man was taboo for a woman.' She adds:

> [Anne's] sense of self, and self-awareness, is what makes her modern to us. She was a woman exercising conscious choice. She controlled her cash and her body. At a time when women had to marry, or be looked after by a male relative, and when all their property on marriage passed to their husband, Anne Lister not only dodged the traps of being female, she set up a liaison with another woman that enhanced her own wealth and left both of them free to live as they wished … . The diaries gave me courage.

Katherine Bradley (1846 – 1914) and Edith Emma Cooper (1862 – 1913)

Irish poet Katherine Harris Bradley and her niece Edith Emma Cooper were lesbian lovers for forty years. Acquaintances of Oscar Wilde, they were well educated (Katherine studied at Newham College, Cambridge – a startling feat considering the attitudes towards women and education), and together they wrote under the pseudonym Michael Field.

Henry Wharton published a translation of the works of the archaic Greek poet Sappho in 1885 which the two women claimed was an inspiration for their literary endeavours. Their substantial co-written diaries can be found in the British Museum. Co-authors of eight books of poetry and twenty-seven plays, their first work, *Callirrhoe: Fair Rosamund* (1884) was well received in Victorian literary circles.

Tobacco heiress Katherine lived with her sister Emma, later taking on the mantle of warden for Emma's daughter Edith. A shared love of literature grew into something much stronger, despite the sixteen-year age gap. Again, proving that financial independence meant a life of sexual freedom, their money seemed to shield them from public approbation, whilst their literary works contained themes of feminine love and eroticism.

Edith Emma Cooper (above) and Katherine Bradley (below).

Poet and friend Robert Browning declared Michael Field a genius and referred to Katherine and Edith as his 'two dear Greek women'. When questioned about the need to write under an assumed name, Katherine told him that society would never accept a poet who wrote about the sexual love between two women.

Feeling more comfortable under the disguise, she and her niece were able to portray women in a more realistic light, even though it was presumably from a male point of view. They also wrote and championed women's rights when it was very dangerous to do so.

Both women died from cancer within a year of each other, with Katherine outliving Emma.

Their legacy is assured, according to Margaret D. Stetz, the Mae and Robert Carter Professor of Women's Studies at the University of Delaware:

> After many years of neglect, these two writers are being studied all around the world. People find them fascinating, because they broke every rule in sight. In the late 19th century, women weren't supposed to attend universities, but the 'Michael Fields' did. Women weren't supposed to be authorities on the Greek Classics, but these two women were. Respectable women weren't supposed to have anything to do with the stage, but they wrote plays and had one of their works produced. English Protestants weren't supposed to be attracted to other religions, but they both converted to Roman Catholicism. And, women certainly weren't supposed to love each other passionately, but they did.

Charlotte Cushman (1816 – 1876)

Known to her adoring public as 'Our Charlotte', Ms Cushman was a nineteenth-century American theatrical actress and descendant of the original pilgrim Robert Cushman.

Charlotte Cushman, photographed by George Kendall Warren, Boston Public Library, c. 1859–1870.

With a vocal range that included the full contralto register, she was famous for playing both female and male roles. Her biographer, Lisa Merrill, describes her as 'a lesbian in an era before some claim the word':

> Cushman challenged Victorian notions of gender in her stage portrayals of male characters and of strong, androgynous female characters. Offstage, she was a powerful businesswoman who supported her family, women lovers, and friends.

Born in Massachusetts, she made her debut performance in a Boston company in 1835, playing Countess Almaviva in *The Marriage of Figaro*. A year later she played Lady Macbeth. American poet and journalist Walt Whitman praised the 'towering grandeur of her genius' in his columns for *The Brooklyn Daily Eagle*. She performed before Queen Victoria, who watched Cushman play Katherine in *Henry VIII* in 1848.

She played more than thirty male characters. The mysterious old gypsy Meg Merrilies in *Guy Mannering* was her most famous role, followed by Lady Macbeth, Queen Katherine, and Nancy in the dramatisation of *Oliver Twist*. She also won praise for playing Romeo, Cardinal Wolsey, and Hamlet.

During 1854 and 1855, she was in London to play Romeo opposite her own sister Susan as Juliet. (Susan bowed out of acting at the age of 14 when she got married. On discovering she was pregnant, her husband left her, leaving Charlotte to look after her sister; she would later adopt the son Ned.)

She never married and instead, her dramatic love life revolved around women. She lived in Europe for ten years as a couple with English writer and actress Matilda Hays; Elizabeth Barrett Browning referred to their relationship as 'a female marriage'.

While living in Rome, Charlotte established a salon-type community of gay and straight female writers and artists. The History Project's Public Faces, Private Lives exhibition at Boston Library in 1996 described it as 'a group of highly mobile, independent women [who] began enjoying an international transatlantic lifestyle that now seems strikingly modern. These women were respected members of the art world, earned large incomes, and kept company with the intellectual and moneyed elites of the time.'

Other offstage lovers included Rosalie Sully, daughter of artist Thomas Sully, and sculptor Emma Stebbins (they would live together until Stebbins' death). Her relationship with Stebbins led to a jealous Hays suing Cushman for palimony and securing a settlement (the amount undisclosed).

In 1858, Charlotte began a country-wide tour of the US, where theatres pronounced her 'the greatest living tragic actress'.

Emma Crow, the 18-year-old she fell in love with, called her 'little lover' and brought her back to Italy. In a bid to conceal their lesbian relationship, Emma married Charlotte's adopted son Ned in 1861.

When she eventually retired in 1875, theatre historian Charles H. Shattuck says Charlotte was awarded 'the most spectacular farewell ceremony in the history of the American theatre, surrounded by civic, literary and theatrical notables.' He adds:

> In a period when most middle-class women were admonished to be passive, submissive, domestic, and, above all, chaste, she endeavoured to support herself, her family, and, later, the women with whom she shared her life through her labor in the sexually charged arena of the stage.

Fashion Victims

Men and women were expected to live very differently from one another, with clearly defined roles regardless of class. However, lift the skirts a little and not only will you see that they didn't wear underwear (women were knickerless until 1800 when they started wearing 'drawers'), they were far less repressed than the stereotypes would have us believe. The Victorians were as weird and wonderful as we are today.

It's hard not to buy into the romanticism of Victorian fashion. Then, of course, one grows up and realises that those enormous gowns acted

Read's Crinoline Sketches, No. 9, 22 July 1859, by anonymous.

as an effective jail warden, keeping women in their place. Trussed up, squeezed tight and unable to perform basic human functions such as breathing, women could barely move, let alone find the energy for emancipation. Victorian women wore a tremendous amount of layers beneath their exquisite gowns: corsets, corset covers, petticoats, bloomers, bustles or crinolines, bust ruffles, garters and suspenders.

And, lest we forget, these fair princesses stank. Not just because of the general disregard at the time for regular bathing, but also after wading through the shit-covered streets with their delicate maiden feet.

Men fared little better. Confined to a strict dress code themselves, there was little space for freedom of thought – a gentleman was never seen in his shirt sleeves, and beards were in and out like a hokey-cokey. If you didn't toe the sartorial line, you were regarded as a skilamalink (a man of shady character).

While men had misogynistic, unrealistic attitudes towards women, they too were subjected to rigid expectations. Women should exude a virginal, aesthetic grace while men had to be providers and moral guardians, and wear their success on the very shirt sleeves they needed to cover up.

The Victorian dress reform, also known as the Rational Dress Movement, proposed wearing clothes that were more practical and comfortable than the fashions at the time. Many women admired the strong heavy-set stability of Queen Victoria as much as they yearned to look like a frail wisp of a fainting damsel.

As we have seen, not all Victorians had a puritanical stick up their backside, and not all women wanted to be trussed up in acres of silk, unable to breathe. Underneath the stiff collars and the starched mountains of petticoats, there still lurked a naked animal with the same instincts as the rest of us. They had as many different ideas of beauty as anyone else, with many women lusting after brooding, immoral and wild Byronic heroes.

Still, all things are not created equal, and there's a good reason why the dress reform movement mainly targeted female clothing.

The story of women, as ever, is more complex than a frivolous and idiotic sex who sacrificed their health for their appearance. They were dressed in a beautifully embroidered prison. In a world where you were forced to base your future security on your partner and his approval, conformity was everything. Rebellious girls, who chose to deviate from the norm fashionwise, risked their marriage prospects – a fate that could land them in the workhouse.

This is not the book if you want to read a detailed description of all the Victorian styles and fripperies; many a detailed account exists that take you on a timeline catwalk. Far more titillating are the disasters, ironies and myths that followed this bountiful time of fashion, the often-ghoulish nature of Victorian dress and the far more frightening similarities to today.

These sexual politics dressed up in cotton and silk add another layer to the tale of Victorian beauty – a story that reads like a gothic tale straight out of a gruesome Penny Dreadful, complete with the horrors of fire-eating crinolines, arsenic-embroidered dresses and throat-puncturing collars that stalked nineteenth-century fashion.

Death was all the rage. From corpse chic to a string of people murdered by their threads, to the Queen's unremitting grief for her husband that inspired a craze for mourning clothes: today's goths would have killed (pun intended) to live in this era.

With short life expectancies, long mourning periods of at least a year were expected. (Side note: the upper classes changed their clothes about six times a day.) Following the death of her beloved Prince Albert in December 1861, Victoria dressed in black for the remaining forty years of her life.

Tuberculosis was so rife that it became an obsession for many Victorians and inspired a sickening, beauty trend. Women wanted to look like the victims of consumption. Popular writers, such as Alfred Tennyson, waxed lyrical about how a woman was at her most gorgeous when she was a corpse, as illustrated in this line from his poem *Maud*: 'Pale with the golden beam of an eyelash dead on the cheek.'

A fair maiden's highest compliment may well have been 'Good God woman you look like death!' It's not a great leap to believe that men were responsible for this grisly look because no woman is as easy to control as a dead one.

The Victorian era witnessed 'an increasing aestheticization of tuberculosis that becomes entwined with feminine beauty,' says Carolyn Day, Assistant Professor of History at Furman University in South Carolina:

> Among the upper class, one of the ways people judged a woman's predisposition to tuberculosis was by her attractiveness. That's because tuberculosis enhances those things that are already established as beautiful in women, such as the thinness and pale skin that result from weight loss and the lack of appetite caused by the disease.

So how did one replicate the nearly departed? Chalk-white skin was essential and lead-imbued cosmetics and arsenic helped achieve this look while hastening you to an early death. In a bizarre and grisly twist of irony, women were often forced to apply more and more lead makeup to cover the damage it had already wreaked.

Other ways to achieve the cute cadaver look was to paint thin blue lines to enhance the veins on white skin. And, of course, the thinner the better. The practice of extreme tightening of corsets was most helpful in restricting appetites and led to frequent fainting fits: mashing your lungs with reinforced whalebone had that effect.

As doctors searched for a cure, they recommended sunbathing as a treatment, which led to the popularity in tanning. (And disease, once again, informs our choices full circle as we go back into the shade to avoid skin cancer.)

Lola Montez was a famously scandalous courtesan and Spanish dancer who used her influence to demand reform (Victorian moralists

A display of Victorian-era cosmetics, including cold creams, hair restorer and various oils.

loved her because she gave them so much to be indignant about), especially with regard to corsets. She said:

> Above all things, to avoid, especially when young, the constant pressure of such hard substances as whalebone and steel; for, besides the destruction to beauty, they are liable to produce all the terrible consequences of abscesses and cancers. A young lady should be instructed that she is not to allow even her own hand to press it too roughly.

Portrait of Lola Montez by Southworth & Hawes, 1851.

Montez fascinated and appalled the Victorian community, but as a famous beauty, her advice was sought. Her book, *The Arts of Beauty; Or, Secrets of a Lady's Toilet* published in 1858, featured a recipe for a breast growth serum:

> Tincture of myrrh 1oz
>
> Pimpernel water 4 oz
>
> Elder-flower water 4 oz
>
> Musk 1 gr
>
> Rectified spirits of wine 6 oz

With the resulting tincture to be 'very softly rubbed upon the bosom for five or ten minutes, two or three times a day.'

Montez summed up the cult of consumption most wittily by advising men to entertain their lady love by 'relating the number of your female friends who have died of consumption within a year.'

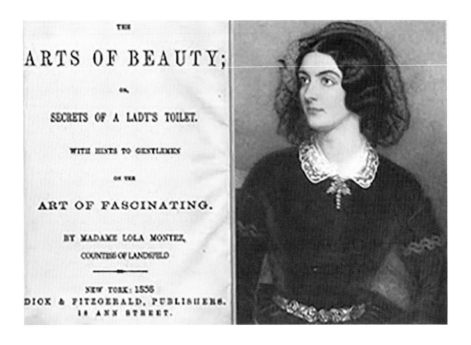

Humour aside, she certainly bought into the zeitgeist of her day, saying: 'Every woman owes it not only to herself, but to society to be as beautiful and charming as she possibly can.'

Certainly, your appearance was effectively your calling card. At a glance it told everyone who you were, how much money you had and how good your prospects were. Position was everything: women had to chase a good husband just to survive. They all knew the dangers of arsenic, belladonna and the like – these were common ingredients in a good old-fashioned Victorian murder – but they didn't care. They were forced to place all their hopes on a decent marriage and if fair looks were created by foul means then so be it.

(Before Botox stops you raising your eyebrows in horror at your ancestors who were happy to drip deadly belladonna in their eyes to look 'pretty' – consider whether anything has changed. If you fast forward to history books in the twenty-second-century, they will have details of how women injected botulinum poison in their face and exploding sacks in their breasts.)

Belladonna was just one of several poisons that graced a Victorian's beauty chest. It was used to create doe eyes by enlarging the pupil, creating a beautiful effect while causing blindness. Some women used lemon juice to achieve the same result.

Mrs S. D. Powers was the period's most famous beauty expert, offering beauty solutions in *The Ugly Papers: Or, Hints for the Toilet* (originally a column in *Harper's Bazaar*). Some were less fatal than others.

Nibbling on Dr Rose's white chalk arsenic wafers, sold by Sears and advertised as 'perfectly harmless', was

Glass bottle used for a tincture of belladonna, 1880–1900. (*Science Museum Group Collection*)

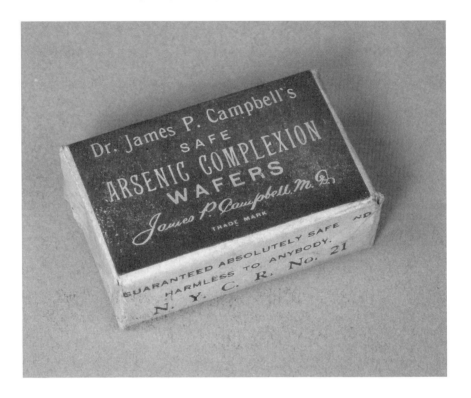

believed to improve the complexion by slowly poisoning the woman, just enough to achieve the sought-after sick, pale and translucent look created by arsenic consumption, without actually causing her to collapse. The whiteness of the skin was also a clear sign that you were well-off enough not to have to labour like a commoner in the sun. Women would also 'enamel' themselves, coating their arms and faces with white paint and enamel to achieve the pale look. Wearing this meant a lady could not express herself facially in case the enamel cracked.

Unsurprisingly, Lola Montez despised the practice, saying, 'If Satan has ever had any direct agency in inducing woman to spoil or deform her own beauty, it must have been in tempting her to use paints and enamelling.'

Mrs Powers advised ladies to use ammonia (also used to clean toilets) as the basis of their beauty regime, describing it as 'the most healthful and efficient stimulus for the hair'. Vermillion aka 'red mercury' was a popular lip tint and poison.

Clothes to Die For

> Let such as see beauty and harmony in distorted spines, compressed lungs, enlarged livers, and displacement of the whole abdominal viscera, together with their sure results, sallow complexion, dull, soulless eyes, trembling limbs, a weary soul in a weary frame – let such seek shelter in their miserable dress-prisons, from the coarse ridicule of *gentlemen* who prefer that woman should be imbecile in body and mind, and from the silly laugh and jeer of women, who deserve not that name.
>
> *The Lily magazine*
> June 1851, Vol III, No 6, p. 47

The corset was an item reviled and desired in equal measure. Desire never wavered for a tiny waist and its subsequent emphasis on hips and boobs, and later, the bottom. The Jessica Rabbit silhouette was alive and kicking – a sartorial expression of sexual desire hidden beneath the chastity belt of a thousand petticoats, steel crinoline cage or the enormous bustle structure which screamed look but don't touch. Or rather, wear but don't move.

The corset shaped the cultural fabric of Victorian society as surely as it squeezed women into an hourglass Barbie of unnatural proportions. Its structure was eye watering:

> The corsets of the 1840s were cut from separate pieces stitched together to give roundness to the bust and shaping over the hips. A broad busk (a flat length of wood or steel) was inserted up the centre front of the corset to give a smooth line to the bodice of the dress. Strips of whalebone were also inserted up the back and sometimes down the side and front, to give more structure. Corsets also had to be rigid to conceal the layers of underwear, including chemise, drawers and petticoat, which were worn underneath.

So important was the corset, its legacy can be seen today in the torrent of English sayings and idioms that flowed from the practice of wearing it. For example, 'heaving bosoms' is a result of the restricted chest and is linked closely with the idea of a distressed damsel; while 'strait laced', refers to a rigid personality.

Girls and young women aimed to have a waist that spanned in inches the same size as their age, i.e. 17 inches if you were 17 years old. To achieve this, some practised what is known as tight lacing. Some mothers even trained young girls with corsets in much the same way as those with bound feet – to keep them petite – were trained from an early age.

Possible dangers of the corset included restricted breathing, organs crushed together, displaced, broken ribs, internal bleeding, chronic gastroesophageal reflux, a propensity to faint, the inability to eat properly and constipation.

In 1903, *The New York Times* reported the news about mother-of-six Mary Halliday. She died of a seizure and the post-mortem showed that two pieces of corset steel had become lodged in her heart. The article said, 'Where they rubbed together the ends were worn to a razor edge by the movement of her body.'

Luckily the Industrial Age and the invention of the sewing machine in 1851 meant clothes could be mass-produced, and working-class women could afford to buy their very own steel traps.

Of course, many women did not practise extreme lacing and wore them far more sensibly. Medical journal *The Lancet* published several articles about the dangers of tight lacing and Mrs S. D. Powers of the *Ugly Papers* fame also decried the practice.

However, there is little doubt that a corset restricted movement and, by extension, a woman's power. And corset wearing left its mark after death: one medical professor warned his students that women who had worn corsets were of no use as cadavers from which to study human anatomy.

The Radical Women's Press of the 1850s referred to women's fashion as 'semi-suicidal', declaring that:

When the day of corsets passed away, there was great commendation, as well there might be, but not at what soon followed. Then came the heavy skirts, bustles, long waists, and longer points, filled with whalebones and other splints fit only to be used on the human frame in case of broken bones. This style of dress has induced more suffering than tightlacing, though that was a more speedy cause of death. One oppressed and displaced important organs, though not the vital; the other attacked the very citadel of life. Both of them are semi-suicidal in their tendency. The excessive heat induced by an inordinate amount of clothing, has caused spinal affections and relaxation of the muscles of the back and abdomen.

Crinolines, stiffened underskirts made using horsehair, in either linen or cotton with a hoop's bell structure, were susceptible to gusts of wind. They were notorious for getting caught in the spokes of carriages and dragging women under. Some were also so ridiculously large that they blocked exits. A particularly perilous affair occurred in Santiago, Chile on 8 December 1863.

A church caught fire after a gas lamp set veils on the wall alight. In the panic to escape, the women got stuck in the doorway when their crinolines blocked the exit like a frilly wall of death. Estimates reckon 2-3,000 people died. Much like the synthetic dressing-up clothes today, hoops positively lit up when exposed to flames.

There was a glut of naked flames in this era. Henry Wadsworth Longfellow's second wife, Mrs Fanny Longfellow, was a famous victim of a crinoline fire, as this report from *The New York Times* illustrates:

> While seated at her library table, making seals for the entertainment of her two youngest children, a match or piece of lighted paper caught her dress, and she was in

Punch magazine, August 1856.

a moment enveloped in flames. Prof. LONGFELLOW, who was in his study, ran to her assistance, and succeeded in extinguishing the flames, with considerable injury to himself, but too late for the rescue of her life. Drs. WYMAN and JOHNSON, of Cambridge, and HENRY J. BIGELOW, of this city, were summoned, and did all that surgical skill could do. Both of the sufferers were under the influence of ether through the night, and yesterday morning Mrs. LONGFELLOW rallied a little, but at 11 o'clock she was forever released from suffering.

Punch magazine advised husbands to insure their wives at fire insurance offices, and there were various suggestions for incombustible dresses.

La crinoline finissant par être soupçonnée, from Actualities, published in *Le Charivari*, 4 July 1857.

Perhaps less well known is the story of Oscar Wilde's Irish half-sisters, Emily and Mary, who died in a terrible tragedy on 10 November 1871 aged just 24 and 22. They were the illegitimate daughters of his father, Sir William Wilde, from Dublin, and lived with their relation, Rev Ralph Wilde, in the county of Monaghan. It is suspected they were kept as their father's dirty secret and their death was little reported, except briefly by the local paper the *Northern Standard*. By all accounts they were lively, popular girls. One can surmise they were in bright moods as they attended a ball at Drumaconnor House, a local manor, looking forward to a night of dancing and merriment.

They had such a good evening they stayed after the last guests had gone to dance a final waltz with their host. But as she whirled around the room, one of the sister's crinolines caught fire from a naked flame in the open fireplace. Her sister rushed to her aid but just ignited her own dress. Their host rushed them outside to roll them in the snow, but it was too late and both girls perished.

The inscription on their headstone in Drumsnat Church reads: 'In memory of two loving and loved sisters … who lost their lives by accident in this parish … . They were lovely and pleasant in their lives and in death they were not divided.'

Some people believe that Oscar Wilde did not even know of their existence. To avoid scandal, Sir William Wilde insisted that no inquest be held, and their names were changed to Wylie in later reports. So, a story that should have burned bright in our history books was relegated to the ashes of a tiny local newspaper.

Amelia Bloomer (1818 – 1894)

> 'Let men be compelled to wear our dress for a while and
> we should soon hear them advocating a change.'

Some women railed against the moral standards and the constrictive clothes of the time. Alas, the story of Amelia Bloomer shows just how hard it was to fight the establishment. A woman's activist fighting for suffrage and reform, she is most famous for adopting and publicising a new style of dress in the 1850s, which was named the bloomer in her honour.

Fighting against the rigidity of women's clothes that gave them so little movement, she publicised the bloomer in *The Lily* in March 1851. It was essentially a pair of baggy trousers, gathered at the ankles worn under a shorter dress or skirt. She wrote:

> As soon as it became known that I was wearing the new dress, letters came pouring in upon me by the hundreds from women all over the country making inquiries about the dress and asking for patterns – showing how ready and anxious women were to throw off the burden of long, heavy skirts.

The bloomer movement was so badly ridiculed by the press and public, it was bullied into submission. Amelia claims she stopped wearing her trousers because of the invention of the crinoline that allowed far greater freedom of movement. However, it is also possible that the attention was so focused on what she wore, that no one paid attention to the women's rights and women's suffrage that she was trying to champion.

Still, many members of the Rational Dress Movement appreciated the physical and political need for Amelia's

Amelia Bloomer

bloomers. They were vehemently against the rib-crushing corset. However, despite their earnest campaigning, a change did not take place until after the invention of the bicycle and the subsequent craze for cycling among the upper classes necessitated a change in dress. Even then, this did not really take root until the Edwardian period.

Men also suffered for fashion; look no further than their neck. It was quite the thing to wear detached collars, attached to the shirts by studs, that were so pointed and starched they became known as a *Vatermorder*: Father Killer.

This meant that should a gentleman, returning from his club a little the worse for wear, sit down to have a nap, and his head were to roll forward, he could choose one of several ways to be killed.

Tight collars could cut off blood supply, lead to asphyxiation or a brain abscess; indigestion could swell the neck leading to a spot of strangulation – its sharpened points were well placed for piercing the jugular.

Mr John Cruetzi got dead drunk in 1888 and fell asleep on a park bench. He was later found as stiff as the collar that killed him. In his obituary, *The New York Times* wrote: 'His head dropped over on his chest and then his stiff collar stopped the windpipe and checked the flow of blood through the already contracted veins, causing the death to ensue from asphyxia and apoplexy.'

Another deadly risk was the use of coloured dyes that contained an arsenic compound. The public was very fearful of them and stories about deadly dresses were a regular feature in magazines and papers leading to the myth of the 'poison green dress'.

Paris Green, one of the deadliest dyes, used in fabric and wallpaper.

Scheele's Green and Paris Green were regarded as the two deadliest dyes. They were used on household items including wallpaper and curtains. The Victorians loved their bright green colour and they were commonly used in paint and wallpaper to keep bugs and beasties away.

A report in the 1890s said that twenty per cent of materials used in dresses contained 3 mg of arsenic per metre. And it wasn't unusual to use at least 7 metres of fabric in your outfit; you don't need to do the maths to know that's a lot of arsenic.

However, dresses rarely touched the skin owing to the thousands of layers worn underneath. A more worrying item was a pair of stockings, which contained a far higher concentration of arsenic and did make contact with the skin. And red and blue dyes were richer in arsenic and far more likely to make you go green around the gills.

As ever, for all the lurid tales of death dresses, it was the lower classes who suffered, not the wealthy women who actually wore the clothes. Factory workers, laundresses, decorators and artisans spent hours exposed to the chemicals and were in real danger.

Where do you suppose Lewis Carroll's Mad Hatter came from? Poisonous chemicals, including mercurous nitrate, were used in the production of felt, causing a veritable feast of reactions for the poor hat makers. Mad hatter disease, or mad hatter syndrome, also known as *erethism* or *erethism mercurialis*, is a neurological disorder which affects the whole central nervous system. Mercury poisoning caused tremors, irritability and pathological shyness, all of which helped coin the witty nickname, which was anything but fun.

Cross Dressing

Thomas Ernest Boulton and Frederick William Park were known to friends as Stella and Fanny. These two Victorian cross-dressers (or transvestites) featured in a famous London trial in 1871, charged with no less than 'conspiring and inciting persons to commit an unnatural offence.' The 'unnatural offence' was sodomy.

Ernest Boulton (left) and Frederick Park as Fanny and Stella, 1869.

Sodomy was not just a grave crime but also an abhorrent sin, as Neil McKenna, Fanny and Stella's biographer explains: 'Its clear associations with excrement lay at the very confluence of potent fears about sex, dirt, disease and death which haunted the national psyche.'

Boulton had previously been arrested for dressing in women's clothing while Park had been accused of being a prostitute. They held normal jobs during the day but dressed as women in the evenings. Boulton had begun a relationship with aristocrat Lord Arthur Pelham-Clinton; the affair was serious enough for Boulton to wear a wedding ring and carry calling cards engraved with 'Lady Stella Pelham-Clinton'.

Having been under police surveillance for a year, on 28 April 1870, while dressed as Fanny and Stella, they were tracked to a party at the Strand Theatre where they were observed flirting with a group of men and even visiting the women's toilets. They were arrested while attempting to leave the venue. Initially charged only with 'personating a woman', further scrutiny of their homes and personal effects led to them being charged with sodomy. They were even subjected to medical examinations to try and prove they'd engaged in the act.

Their lawyer persuaded the jury at their 1871 Old Bailey trial that 'Ernest Boulton was merely a high-spirited young man with a taste for amateur theatricals, and that no sodomite would be so bold as to advertise the fact by running up and down the Strand in a ballgown.'

The trial caused an absolute sensation, with newspapers billing them the 'He-She Ladies'. Stella's lover, Lord Arthur, died before he was due to appear in court. Theories as to his cause of death range from suicide to scarlet fever to faking his death and moving abroad to start a new life.

Boulton and Park were eventually acquitted because of the lack of evidence that men dressing as women was against the law and, perhaps, because the Victorian public couldn't believe two men could be so openly homosexual. The jury took just fifty-three minutes to find them 'not guilty',

Park moved to the US and died in 1881 at the age of 34. Boulton toured as a female impersonator, dying from a brain tumour in 1904 at the age of 56.

Dr James Barry (c. 1789 – 1865)

Dr James Barry was born in Ireland as Margaret Ann Bulkley, daughter to Mary-Ann and greengrocer Jeremiah.

Determined to pursue a medical career, her life changed after her father was imprisoned for debt in 1803. Taken in and helped by her uncle, artist James Barry, whose name she assumed, she lived as a man, sailing from London to Edinburgh in 1809 to earn a degree at the city's medical school.

She had the full support of her mother, who took on the charade of 'aunt' to her 'nephew'.

Dr Barry joined the British Army in 1813 and became surgeon general, serving in India and South Africa. Not one to rest on her

laurels, she was also Inspector General of Hospitals in Canada, and served in Corfu, the Crimea, Mauritius, Jamaica and St Helena. She was posted to South Africa in 1816, became closely acquainted with its governor, Lord Charles Somerset, and mysteriously disappeared for a full year around 1819. This is when some historians believe she gave birth to a presumably stillborn child, before returning to South Africa, where she is credited as being the first British surgeon to perform a

Caesarean section in Africa where both mother and child survived the procedure.

Her disguise was only revealed on her death from dysentery, on 25 July 1865. Her housemaid, Sophia Bishop, tasked with preparing the body for burial, disregarded the deceased's last wishes NOT to undress the body and made her startling discovery.

Such was the incredulity at the news that the British Army sealed all related records for a century. Whether it was because of the scandal of her fooling the establishment for so many years, or the shock that a mere woman had scaled such incredible career heights, is for you to decide. The likelihood of her having conceived a child was given further weight by the fact that the body bore stretch marks, obviously associated with pregnancy and childbirth.

Dr James fought a duel with pistols, was known to speak her mind and got into a war of words with Florence Nightingale, who later wrote of the altercation:

> I never had such a blackguard rating in all my life – I who have had more than any woman – than from this Barry sitting on his horse, while I was crossing the Hospital Square with only my cap on in the sun. He kept me standing in the midst of quite a crowd of soldiers, Commissariat, servants, camp followers, etc., etc., every one of whom behaved like a gentleman during the scolding I received while he behaved like a brute … . After he was dead, I was told that [Barry] was a woman . . . I should say that [Barry] was the most hardened creature I ever met.

Rather ironic, considering they were both passionate about health reform in their own way. Dr James also acquiesced to a request from Napoleon to treat the son of his private secretary.

Dr James Barry was the first woman in Britain to practise medicine, albeit one disguised as a man. It illustrates the extraordinary lengths women were prepared to go to – had to go to – in order to achieve their ambition.

She is buried in Kensal Green Cemetery under the name of James Barry.

John Ruskin and Euphemia 'Effie' Gray

In 1848, Victorian art critic, artist and architect John Ruskin married the beautiful 19-year-old Euphemia Gray.

She had rejected his first proposal of marriage, accepting it only when it became clear that marrying into Ruskin's prosperous family would alleviate her own family's financial woes.

The marriage was not a happy one and after six years, Effie fell in love with her husband's artistic protégé, John Everett Millais (1829 – 1896). While modelling for his painting, *The Order of Release*, (ironically illustrating a stalwart wife handing over release papers for her imprisoned husband), she wrote of him to her mother:

Left, John Ruskin's watercolour self-portrait from *The Works of John Ruskin (1903 – 1912)*, National Gallery; right, John Everett Millais' self-portrait.

Effie Gray in middle age, portrait by Millais.

'Millais is so extremely handsome, besides his talents, that you may fancy how he is run after.'

It has been argued that Ruskin was duped – that he genuinely married for love (knowing Effie for years before they wed) while she, with her father on the brink of bankruptcy, married for financial gain. He said: 'I married like a fool, because a girl's face pleased me. She married me for my money, breaking her faith to a poor lover.'

He is said to have advised waiting six years before attempting to consummate the marriage – to give his wife time to grow to love him. She presented herself to him naked on their wedding night, but it was never consummated. Rumours abound to this day. Was he secretly gay? Was he horrified by the sight of her pubic hair, his only previous encounters with the female body having been from studying the smooth form of Greek statues. Did she have extreme body odour? Even paedophilia was suggested, following details of a letter he wrote to his doctor John Simon in 1886:

> I like my girls from 10 to 16 – allowing of 17 or 18 as long as they're not in love with anybody but me. I've got some darlings of eight, 12, 14 just now, and my Pigwiggina here – 12 – who fetches my wood and is learning to play my bells.

On a trip to Venice, Effie was left to her own devices whilst Ruskin worked on his book *The Stones of Venice*. She attracted several admirers amongst the soldiers stationed there, even writing that 'Venice is so tempting just now at night that it is hardly possible not to be imprudent.' They are hardly the words of an unworldly shy naive young woman; indeed, her confidence led to two soldiers fighting a duel over her – one of them dying as a result, and Ruskin himself being challenged to another, which he refused.

Ruskin encouraged Effie's intimacy with Millais, inviting him to join them on a holiday in Scotland in 1853. He persuaded her father that news of a divorce would be so scandalous that petitioning for annulment based on non-consummation was the best step.

The story riveted and shocked Victorian England. Gossip around the affair was salacious. Responding to allegations that he was appalled by her body hair and could not consummate the marriage, he said, rather savagely:

> It may be thought strange that I could abstain from a woman who to most people was so attractive. But though

her face was beautiful, her person was not formed to excite passion. On the contrary, there were certain circumstances in her person which completely checked it.

It's a claim that Ruskin biographer Robert Hewison dismisses: 'The whole pubic hair nonsense is like a great big wall preventing people understanding Ruskin. The idea that he did not know what women looked like is a nonsense. It is frankly irritating.'

We may never know the truth as the bulk of the correspondence between the two was destroyed by Effie's family, probably to protect her reputation.

We do know that Effie remarked:

> He alleged various reasons, hatred to children, religious motives, a desire to preserve my beauty, and, finally this last year he told me his true reason ... that he had imagined women were quite different to what he saw I was, and that the reason he did not make me his wife was because he was disgusted with my person the first evening.

According to Robert Brownell in his book *Marriage of Inconvenience*:

> Ruskin was willing to take the stigma of non-consummation on himself because he wouldn't be medically examined and nor were annulments usually reported in the press. If Effie's father had helped dupe Ruskin into the marriage, he was in turn duped into ending it. Ruskin used the threat of divorce and the ensuing scandal to pressurise Mr Gray into persuading Effie to instigate annulment proceedings instead. The ruse worked. Two doctors attested to Effie's virginity, Ruskin himself was out of the country at the time, and in 1854 the marriage was officially ended.

Effie went on to marry Millais and have eight children with him; Ruskin's attempt to move on and woo another young woman, Rosa La Touche, (he proposed when she was 18) was destroyed by Effie bad-mouthing him to her parents. Queen Victoria, appalled at the entire affair, refused to receive Effie at court. Ruskin, a contemporary of Turner and Lewis Carroll, was the first Slade Professor of Fine Art at Oxford, with Ruskin College named after him. Greg Wise, the actor who played the part of Ruskin in the film *Effie*, says that admirers view the marriage 'as a six-year hiccup in the great man's progress'.

Marriage and Divorce

Forget internet dating, casual hook ups and one-night stands. Betrothment in the Victorian era was a serious business, with emphasis on the 'business' side of things. A suitor took courting seriously – as the property of whomever he chose as a bride would revert to him upon marriage.

Queen Victoria and Albert re-enact their wedding ceremony, c. 1854, around fourteen years after they married.

Until 1823 the legal age for men and women to marry in England was 21. After that time, a boy could marry as young as 14, and a girl as young as 12. Most women married between the ages of 18 and 23; any older and you were considered a spinster. Their grooms were usually five years older.

As ever, there was a difference between how the various social classes would court. Lower classes would meet at church or local dances; proper young ladies would meet prospective suitors at balls and 'coming out' dances.

If you were young, single and female, you could forget leaving the house on your own, especially if there were men in the social group. It wasn't going to happen – not without a chaperone, preferably a married one.

Sex before marriage was out of the question. Not for a respectable young lady. Any whiff of scandal would seriously impede a young lady's reputation. She had to be an innocent in all things and only be interested in marriage as a means of being a good upstanding woman and having a family. She wasn't even permitted to speak to a man unless a married woman was present to act as a chaperone or to properly introduce them. A woman could also not receive a social call from a gentleman at home without a family member being present. Any physical contact prior to marriage was forbidden; they could, however, upon being formally engaged, hold hands, as Kathryn Hughes explains:

> If a young man was particularly pious, he might manage to stay chaste until he married. Many respectable young men, however, resorted to using prostitutes. All the major cities had red light districts where it was easy to find a woman whom you could pay for sex. Out-of-towners could consult such volumes as Roger Funnyman's *The Swell's Night Guide Through the Metropolis*. Unfortunately, syphilis and other sexual diseases were rife, and many

young men unwittingly passed on the infection to their wives. For those unlucky enough to develop full-blown tertiary syphilis, the result was a painful and lingering death, usually in the mid-40s.

In Charles Petrie's article, 'Victorian Women Expected to be Idle and Ignorant', he explains exactly what the Victorian man was looking for:

> Innocence was what he demanded from the girls of his class, and they must not only be innocent but also give the outward impression of being innocent. White muslin, typical of virginal purity, clothed many a heroine, with delicate shades of blue and pink next in popularity. The stamp of masculine approval was placed upon ignorance of the world, meekness, lack of opinions, general helplessness and weakness; in short, recognition of female inferiority to the male.

Upon marriage, a woman's property would automatically be owned by her new husband; with wives entirely financially dependent upon them. Bizarrely, one of the few 'rights' granted to women was the ability to refuse sex if their husband could not achieve 'mutual adjustment', that is 'the orgasm of the woman and the ejaculation of semen of the man in the same instant.'

The upper classes had a very casual outlook towards marriage, which allowed both sides to pursue extra-marital relations as long as they followed a specific 'code' of behaviour, namely keeping up appearances, and keeping any affairs out of the newspapers and out of the divorce courts. Affairs were commonplace and fitted into a lady's daily schedule:

> Affairs were conducted in Victorian style with weekend house parties in labyrinthine mansions, golden afternoons

on immaculate green lawns with croquet, tea and cucumber sandwiches, tiny smiles during dinner, adjoining bedrooms. It was, along with hunting, shooting, fishing and charitable works, one of the ways in which those who did not have to work for a living could fill their afternoons. The term 'adultery' applied only to married women, who were more likely than unmarried women to pass the hours between five and seven (the 'cinq a sept') in the pattern set by the Prince of Wales. The choice for this hour of day was purely practical. It took considerable time for a lady to unbutton and unlace her layers of corsets and underskirts, let alone button and lace them up again. Lovers therefore visited just after tea, when ladies were undressing to change their afternoon clothes for their evening ones.

Once a wife had produced at least an heir and a spare, she could, providing she avoided scandal, step away from her husband's bed and embark on discreet liaisons. You could do largely what you liked, within reason, as long as you weren't found out.

It was virtually impossible to be as good as the Victorians pretended to be, but the grim fate that had befallen the French aristocracy was still within living memory, and that was enough to convince their British counterparts that they should keep their own peccadilloes and extravagances well hidden. Fear that the press would foment unrest among the labouring masses upon whom their incomes and comforts depended made them pretend to a quite unrealistic degree of piety and decorum, while secretly indulging their vices just as they had always done … love affairs were therefore conducted with discretion and dignity. No careless female hand might brush the shoulder of the man who had spent most of the previous night in her bed, nor were endearments permitted in public.

In nineteenth-century England, an actual Act of Parliament was necessary to end a marriage. (Only 325 divorces had been granted since 1670.) The 1857 Matrimonial Causes Act made divorce much easier to come by. The husband had to prove adultery and the wife had to prove cruelty and adultery. Women had to be extra careful as, according to Michelle Legro, 'A woman's adultery was considered more serious because she could produce a bastard heir.'

Caroline Norton (1808 – 1877)

The fighting force behind the changes in legislation, which set a tone for reforming the rights of Victorian women, was Caroline Norton.

She was born Caroline Sheridan on 22 March 1808, into a genteel but financially challenged family. Against her better instincts, she was pushed into a marriage with George Norton in order to secure her family's fortunes.

The marriage was not a happy one, with Norton, then the Tory MP for Guildford, physically abusing her regularly. While he proved to be completely unworthy of his job and was deselected at the next election, Caroline, who was extremely intelligent and an accomplished writer, busied herself with work, published poetry, was appointed editor of two society publications and became a popular society hostess.

She gave birth to sons Fletcher in 1829 and Thomas in 1831. When she was heavily pregnant with William (born in 1833), George beat her up and pushed her down a flight of stairs; the servants had to intervene in order to save her life. Three years later it happened again, and this time she miscarried. This, and the semblance of financial independence her work afforded her, gave her the impetus to leave Norton in 1836.

Lithograph of Caroline Norton, c. 1836. Publisher not identified. (*Wellcome Library*)

This was a brave move considering wives had no rights; a factor brought home to her when George stole her children.

> Fletcher, Thomas and William were all snatched up and sent to his relatives in Scotland and Yorkshire. Caroline had no legal recourse. In fact, the law was entirely on

George's side. Only the father of children had any rights to them under the law at that time. Caroline didn't even have the right to visit her children, and it would be many long years before she saw any of them again.

George retaliated again. Although Caroline's only income was the royalties from her books, George sued and won them himself. 'A wife had no legal right to property or earnings – all money she earned belonged to her husband. Caroline was left with nothing.'

Convinced that Caroline had committed adultery with William Lamb aka Prime Minister Lord Melbourne, George also sued him for 'criminal conversation' with Caroline.

The image below is a coloured lithograph from around 1836. It depicts a woman holding a lamb in her lap while a ram looks on and it represents Caroline Norton, her relationship with William Lamb, Lord Melbourne, and the disaffection of her husband.

Not content with what this would mean for both Caroline and Melbourne's reputation, Norton took out newspaper adverts denouncing her and dangled the promise of allowing her visitation rights to their children if she took his side in the trial. Caroline refused and after nine days, the case was thrown out of court.

In 1837 she published *Separation of Mother and Child by the Laws of Custody of Infants Considered*, with case studies of women who had their rights to their children violently disabused by their husbands.

> She pointed out that though wives were thinking, breathing, intelligent people, in the eyes of the law they were as much their husband's property as a brood-mare

or a stretch of land he might purchase. She ended with an appeal to the lawmakers, that 'for the peace of society, and the credit of humanity', they should admit the mother's right to her children to be considered.

Her fight to overturn these injustices, which included a letter to the Queen, played a large part in the passing of the Infant Custody Bill of 1839. It meant that although men were automatically given custody, women could appeal if the child was under the age of 7 and gain access if the child was older.

Vindictive to the end, Norton had their sons sent to Scotland, where the new law wouldn't apply. And it was there that her youngest son William died before she could get to him, from blood poisoning following a fall from a horse. After this Norton awarded Caroline custody of Fletcher and Thomas. She continued to fight for justice for women in abusive relationships as well as for divorce law reform, even giving a powerful testimony in Parliament in 1855. Her efforts led to the Matrimonial Causes Act in 1857, which meant that divorce no longer needed an actual act of Parliament, but could be granted by civil divorce courts. The impact of the new act meant that 300 petitions for divorce were presented in the first year of its passing.

Subsequent divorce reporting in the press, such as *The Times*, led to Queen Victoria imploring the chief designer of the Divorce Act to put a lid on some of the more scandalous stories, as 'none of the worst French novels from which careful parents try to protect their children can be as bad as what is daily brought and laid upon the breakfast table of every educated family in England.'

Isabella Robinson

Isabella Robinson's diary (the original of which no longer exists) created a Victorian scandal comparable to Flaubert's Madame Bovary.

She became one of the first women to be subjected to the new divorce law courts of 1857, championed by Caroline Norton.

Her diary entries reveal the Victorian attitudes of one rule for men and another for women. Her civil engineer second husband Henry was described as an 'uncongenial partner', 'uneducated', 'selfish' and 'harsh-tempered', and he fathered two children with his mistress. He also spent freely from her bank account, which he had taken control of upon their marriage.

Thirty-seven-year-old Isabella meanwhile, as detailed in the diary, was desperate for both sexual and intellectual stimulation and embarked on an affair with 27-year-old married family friend Dr Edward Lane. She detailed every bit of it although there is an argument that was pure fantasy and the 'affair' didn't happen at all.

As fate would have it, Henry discovered the diary, took their children and used the diary's contents in court, and across the press, as evidence against her as he sued for divorce in the new Court of Divorce and Matrimonial Causes at Westminster Hall, London, on 14 June 1858. As one report says:

> The court proceedings make for disturbing but engrossing reading. The contents of Isabella's diary were divulged to the lawyers and judges and reprinted in the newspapers. Her innermost feelings, wishes and dreams were revealed at breakfast tables across the country. And, as if her situation weren't awful enough, her lawyers argued that she was a sex maniac who had created an imaginary erotic life.

Since the diary was Henry's only proof of his wife's adultery, her lawyers insisted that parts of it were fictional – a result of her 'uterine disease', which had caused temporary insanity. Medical experts confirmed that her condition could cause sexual delusions and nymphomania. The newspapers gorged on every detail.

A Victorian divorce court, c. 1870. Isabella Robinson was not allowed to appear as a witness for her defence; her only voice in court was her diary.

Isabella won the court case by also claiming the diary was a complete work of fiction. Dr Lane, perhaps to preserve his own reputation and livelihood, described her as 'a vile and crazy woman' who was 'goaded on by wild hallucinations'.

With the court refusing to allow grounds for divorce, Isabella remained married and retained access to her allowance and her children. In 1864, she was caught with her children's French tutor – and Henry Robinson finally got the divorce he so desperately wanted.

Past and Present – the first of a set of three modern-life pictures on the theme of the fallen woman, by Augustus Leopold Egg.

This painting, in which a husband discovers his wife's adultery in a letter, was part of a moralising triptych exhibited at the Royal Academy just weeks before the Robinson trial.

Princess Louise, the Duchess of Argyll (1848 – 1939)

In the search for scandalous Victorians, one doesn't need to look much further than Princess Louise, the sixth child and fourth daughter of Victoria and Albert themselves.

Louise trained as a sculptor (her marble statue of her mother can be seen in Kensington Gardens) and rebelled in a fashion by being the only one of her sisters to not marry into royalty. Instead, she chose Lord Lorne, later Duke of Argyll. The marriage was unhappy and childless, with enduring rumours that the duke was gay.

There were whispers of a scandalous illegitimate child, which Louise allegedly gave birth to when she was just 18 years old. The father was rumoured to have been Walter Stirling, tutor to Princess Louise's brother Prince Leopold.

This rumour originated with the family of Sir Charles Locock, who was Queen Victoria's obstetrician and delivered all her nine babies. Locock had a son named Frederick, and in 1867 Frederick adopted a baby boy called Henry. When Henry grew up, he told all his children that his mother was Princess Louise.

Official engagement photograph of Princess Louise & Marquess of Lorne, W. & D. Downey, 1870.

In 2004, his descendants applied for permission to take a sample of Henry's DNA from his coffin in order to compare it with the DNA of Louise's niece, the Tzarina Alexandra of Russia. Permission was refused by the Court of Arches.

There are also rumours that Louise had an affair with sculptor Edgar Boehm, who died while *in flagrante* with the princess. Princess Louise died at the grand old age of 91, owing fifteen shillings to a London tobacconist. She left around £70 million in her will.

References

Child Labour

Match Girls
www.bbc.co.uk/legacies/work/england/london/article_1.shtml
www.theheroinecollective.com/the-match-girls/
www.mentalfloss.com/article/79545/matchsticks-once-sickened-and-deformed-women-and-children

Sex and Perversion

www.vam.ac.uk/content/articles/s/sex-and-sexuality-19th-century/

Masturbation and Erotica
www.mentalfloss.com/article/32042/corn-flakes-were-invented-part-anti-masturbation-crusade
Riddell, Fern, *The Victorian Guide to Sex: Desire and Deviance in the 19th Century*, (Pen and Sword 2014)
http://pictorial.jezebel.com/john-harvey-kelloggs-legacy-of-cereal-sociopathy-and-1777402050
www.standard.co.uk/lifestyle/this-longlost-study-on-victorian-sex-teaches-a-very-modern-lesson-a3340276.html
www.vam.ac.uk/content/articles/s/sex-and-sexuality-19th-century/

Pornography
www.makingqueerhistory.com/articles/2018/9/23/algernon-charles-swinburne

www.valentinagurarie.wordpress.com/2016/02/19/10-popular-erotic-books-of-19th-century/

www.silkensheetsandseduction.wordpress.com/2011/10/21/bdsm-in-the-victorian-era/

Terrot, Charles, *Traffic in Innocents: The Shocking Story of White Slavery in England,* (New York E. P. Dutton & Co 1960) p. 91, via www.bestslavetraining.com

Swinburne, Algernon, C., *The Whippingham Papers,* (Wordsworth Classics 1995) via

www.the-toast.net/2014/04/10/pearl-victorian-porn-finest/

www.theguardian.com/science/blog/2017/oct/16/itvs-victoria-illustrates-how-19th-century-sexism-helped-syphilis-to-spread

Prostitution and the Fallen Woman

www.bl.uk/romantics-and-victorians/articles/prostitution

Nolland, Lisa S., *A Victorian Feminist Christian: Josephine Butler, the Prostitutes and God*, (Paternoster Press 2005) pp. 71-72

www.warwick.ac.uk/fac/cross_fac/iatl/reinvention/archive/volume1issue1/joyce/

www.sites.udel.edu/britlitwiki/victorian-prostitution/In Good Stead

www.coventgardenmemories.org.uk/page/wt_stead

Jack the Ripper

www.theguardian.com/books/2019/mar/01/hallie-rubenhold-jack-the-ripper-victims

Oscar Wilde

www.anothermag.com/art-photography/9012/how-oscar-wilde-paved-the-way-for-gay-rights-in-the-arts

www.theguardian.com/uk/2001/may/06/books.booksnews

Scandal of 19 Cleveland Street

www.clevelandstreetscandal.com/

REFERENCES

Anne Lister of Shibden Hall

www.historyextra.com/period/victorian/anne-lister-real-gentleman-jack-diary-code-history-secret-life-britain-first-modern-lesbian/

Cawthorne, Ellie writing for *BBC History* magazine, in conversation with Angela Steidele, author of *Gentleman Jack: A Biography of Anne Lister, Regency Landowner, Seducer and Secret Diarist*, (Serpent's Tail, 2018)

www.rictornorton.co.uk/lister.htm

www.bbc.co.uk/news/resources/idt-sh/the_life_and_loves_of_anne_lister

www.refinery29.com/en-us/2019/04/230512/anne-lister-ann-walker-marriage-true-story-gentleman-jack

www.jeanettewinterson.com/journalism/about-anne-lister/

Katherine Bradley and Edith Emma Cooper

sappho.com/poetry/m_field.html

www.justaboutwrite.com/Herstory-Poet-MichaelField.html

www.poetryfoundation.org/poets/michael-field

Charlotte Cushman

Merrill, Lisa, *When Romeo Was a Woman: Charlotte Cushman and Her Circle of Female Spectators*, (University of Michigan Press, 2000)

Wojczuk, Tana, *Lady Romeo: The Radical and Revolutionary Life of Charlotte Cushman*, (Simon & Schuster 2020)

www.biography.yourdictionary.com/charlotte-cushman

www.historyproject.org/exhibition/public-faces-private-lives

www.folger.edu/shakespeare-unlimited/romeo-charlotte-cushman

www.bl.uk/collection-items/lithograph-of-the-cushman-sisters-as-romeo-and-juliet

www.newenglandhistoricalsociety.com/charlotte-cushman-cross-dressing-tragedienne-of-the-19th-century/

Fashion Victims

www.kristinholt.com/archives/5331

www.smithsonianmag.com/science-nature/how-tuberculosis-shaped-victorian-fashion-180959029/

www.theweek.com/articles/458466/how-grow-bosom-according-100yearold-beauty-books

www.atlasobscura.com/articles/the-poisonous-beauty-advice-columns-of-victorian-england

Clothes To Die For

www.vam.ac.uk/content/articles/c/corsets-and-crinolines-in-victorian-fashion/?gclid=EAIaIQobChMIm9aNm4n65wIVx7TtCh19mwXMEAAYASAAEgI58fD_BwE

Russo, Ann and Kramarae, Cheris, *The Radical Women's Press of the 1850s* (Routledge 1991)

www.nytimes.com/1861/07/12/archives/the-death-of-mrs-longfellow.html

Amelia Bloomer

www.thedailybeast.com/corsets-muslin-disease-and-more-of-the-deadly-fashion-trends

Cross Dressing

McKenna, Neil, *Fanny and Stella: The Young Men who Shocked Victorian England* (Faber & Faber 2013), p. 272

www.victorianlondon.org/women/crossdressing.htm

www.history.howstuffworks.com/historical-figures/scandal-cross-dressing-men-victorian-england.htm

Dr James Barry

Du Preez, Michael and Dronfield, Jeremy, *Dr James Barry, A Woman Ahead of Her Time'*, (One World 2016), p. 340

John Ruskin and Euphemia 'Effie' Gray

Brownell, Robert *Marriage of Inconvenience*, (Pallas Athene 2014) via

www.theguardian.com/film/2010/mar/14/john-ruskin-wedding-effie-gray

www.artuk.org/discover/stories/the-secret-lives-of-two-scandalous-victorian-marriages

Marriage and Divorce

Hughes, Kathryn, 'Gender and Sexuality', (15 May 2014) featured online at the British Library: www.bl.uk/romantics-and-victorians/articles/gender-roles-in-the-19th-century

Petrie, Charles in Swisher, Clarice, *Victorian England* (Greenhaven Press 2000), p. 178

www.faena.com/aleph/articles/the-comical-victorian-myths-on-sexuality/

www.enoughofthistomfoolery.wordpress.com/2015/07/23/rules-of-the-game-love-courtship-marriage-sex-and-married-life-from-the-19th-century-until-1939-part-3-adultery-and-infidelity/

www.literary-liaisons.com/article009.html

www.theguardian.com/books/2013/jan/26/family-secrets-deborah-cohen-review

www.salon.com/2014/09/15/the15_most_bizarre_sex_tips_from_the_victorian_era_partner/

Caroline Norton

www.headstuff.org/culture/history/terrible-people-from-history/caroline-norton-poet-feminist/

Isabella Robinson

Summerscale, Kate, *Mrs Robinson's Disgrace: Tracing the Evolution of Women's Rights in a Victorian Lady's Journals*

(Bloomsbury 2013) via www.brainpickings.org/2012/06/22/mrs-robinsons-disgrace/

www.historytoday.com/blog/2012/09/private-diary-victorian-lady

www.npr.org/2012/06/19/154766639/divorce-disgrace-and-one-steamy-victorian-diary

www.historytoday.com/reviews/private-diary-victorian-lady

www.nytimes.com/2012/06/24/books/review/mrs-robinsons-disgrace-by-kate-summerscale.html

Princess Louise, Duchess of Argyll

www.spectator.co.uk/2014/01/the-mystery-of-princess-louise-by-lucinda-hawksley-review/

Bibliography

Brownell, Robert *Marriage of Inconvenience*, (Pallas Athene 2014)

Du Preez, Michael and Dronfield, Jeremy, *Dr James Barry, A Woman Ahead of Her Time*, (One World 2016)

McKenna, Neil, *Fanny and Stella: The Young Men who Shocked Victorian England*, (Faber & Faber 2013)

Merrill, Lisa, *When Romeo Was a Woman: Charlotte Cushman and Her Circle of Female Spectators*, (University of Michigan Press 2000)

Montez, Lola, *The Arts of Beauty; Or, Secrets of a Lady's Toilet*, (Dick & Fitzgerald 1858)

Nolland, Lisa S., *A Victorian Feminist Christian: Josephine Butler, the Prostitutes and God*, (Paternoster Press 2005)

ONeill Therese, *Unmentionable: The Victorian Lady's Guide to Sex, Marriage and Manners*, (Little, Brown 2016)

Riddell, Fern, *The Victorian Guide to Sex: Desire and Deviance in the 19th Century*, (Pen and Sword 2014)

Rubenhold, Hallie, *The Five: The Untold Lives of the Women Killed by Jack the Ripper*, (Doubleday 2019)

Russo, Ann and Kramarae, Cheris, *The Radical Women's Press of the 1850s* (Routledge 1991)

Steidele, Angela, *Gentleman Jack: A Biography of Anne Lister* (Serpent's Tail 2018)

Summerscale, Kate, *Mrs Robinson's Disgrace, The Private Diary of a Victorian Lady,* (Bloomsbury 2013)

Swinburne, Charles A., *The Whippingham Papers*, (Wordsworth Editions 1995)

Swisher, Clarice, *Victorian England* (Greenhaven Press 2000)

Terrot, Charles, *Traffic in Innocents: The Shocking Story of White Slavery in England,* (Dutton 1960)

Vicinus, Martha, *Intimate Friends: Women Who Loved Women, 1778 – 1928,* (University of Chicago Press 2004)

Walkowitz, Judith, *Prostitution and Victorian Society,* (Cambridge University Press 1980)

Wojczuk, Tana, *Lady Romeo: The Radical and Revolutionary Life of Charlotte Cushman,* (Simon & Schuster 2020)